THE
PEAK
DISTRICT

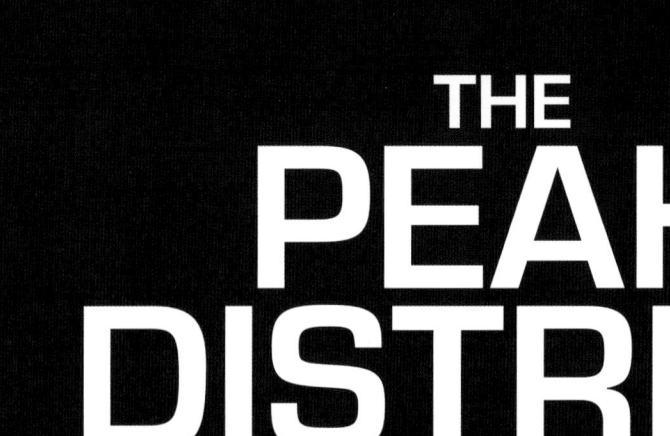

First published in Great Britain in 2011

Copyright © Chris Herring 2011

All rights reserved. No part of this publication may be reproduced, stored in a retrieval system, or transmitted in any form or by any means without the prior permission of the copyright holder.

British Library Cataloguing-in-Publication Data
A CIP record for this title is available from the British Library

ISBN 978 1 84114 917 2

HALSGROVE
Halsgrove House,
Ryelands Business Park,
Bagley Road, Wellington,
Somerset TA21 9PZ
Tel: 01823 653777
Fax: 01823 216796
email: sales@halsgrove.com

Part of the Halsgrove group of companies. Information on all Halsgrove titles is available at: www.halsgrove.com

Printed and bound in China by
Everbest Printing Co Ltd

INTRODUCTION

The Peak District is an area of great natural beauty made up of rocky outcrops, peat-covered moorlands and wonderful limestone dales. The Peak District is predominantly split into two distinctive areas the White Peak and the Dark Peak. The Dark Peak generally consists of high gritstone moorland with rugged outcrops and ledges whereas the White Peak generally consists of a gentler landscape made up of limestone dales and meadows.

The Peak District National Park itself was formed in 1951 and became the first national park in Britain. Because of its close proximity to the large cities of Manchester and Sheffield and with excellent road and rail links it is the most visited national park in the country.

The varied landscape and the changeable weather and light make the Peak District a dream to photograph for the landscape photographer. I feel the panoramic format is particularly well suited to the area and whilst gathering images for this book I purposely shot the majority of images over a twelve month period to show how the landscape of the Peak District dramatically changes throughout the seasons.

I have photographed many areas of the UK, but the Peak District has to be one of my favourites. The Peak District can be a strange place to capture at times as you can feel extremely isolated in a remote and wild landscape yet at the same time the cities of Manchester and Sheffield are just a short drive away. I think the variety of the scenery of the Peak District is what also lures me back time and time again. I love waking up at dawn and heading out with the morning light painting the surrounding landscape. The Peak District has so much to offer that even if I photographed the area over a lifetime there would still be plenty of new places to see and explore.

I must admit I was rather fortunate whilst gathering winter images for this book following one of the finest spells I have witnessed in the Peak District with plenty of heavy snow and wonderful winter light. With all the images I shoot, light and atmosphere are paramount to the success of the images and because of this I can often be found wandering around in the freezing cold at some ridiculous hour of the morning waiting for the sun to rise.

The choice of images throughout this book is entirely personal but I hope they will take you on a photographic journey showcasing the extraordinary light and landscape of the beautiful Peak District.

After a clear night following days of heavy rain a fabulous mist invades the valley beneath Froggatt Edge at first light on a spring morning in May 2010.

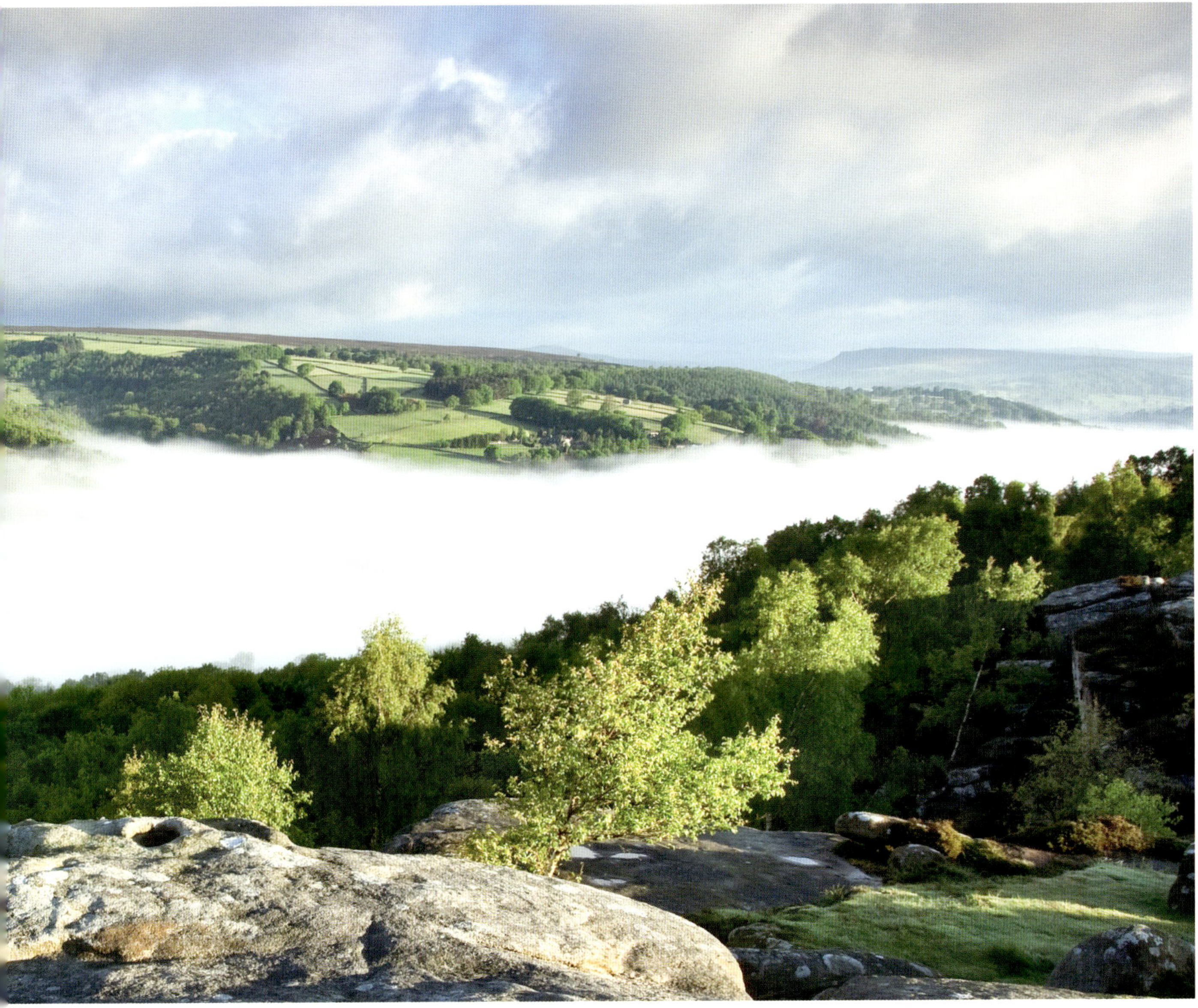

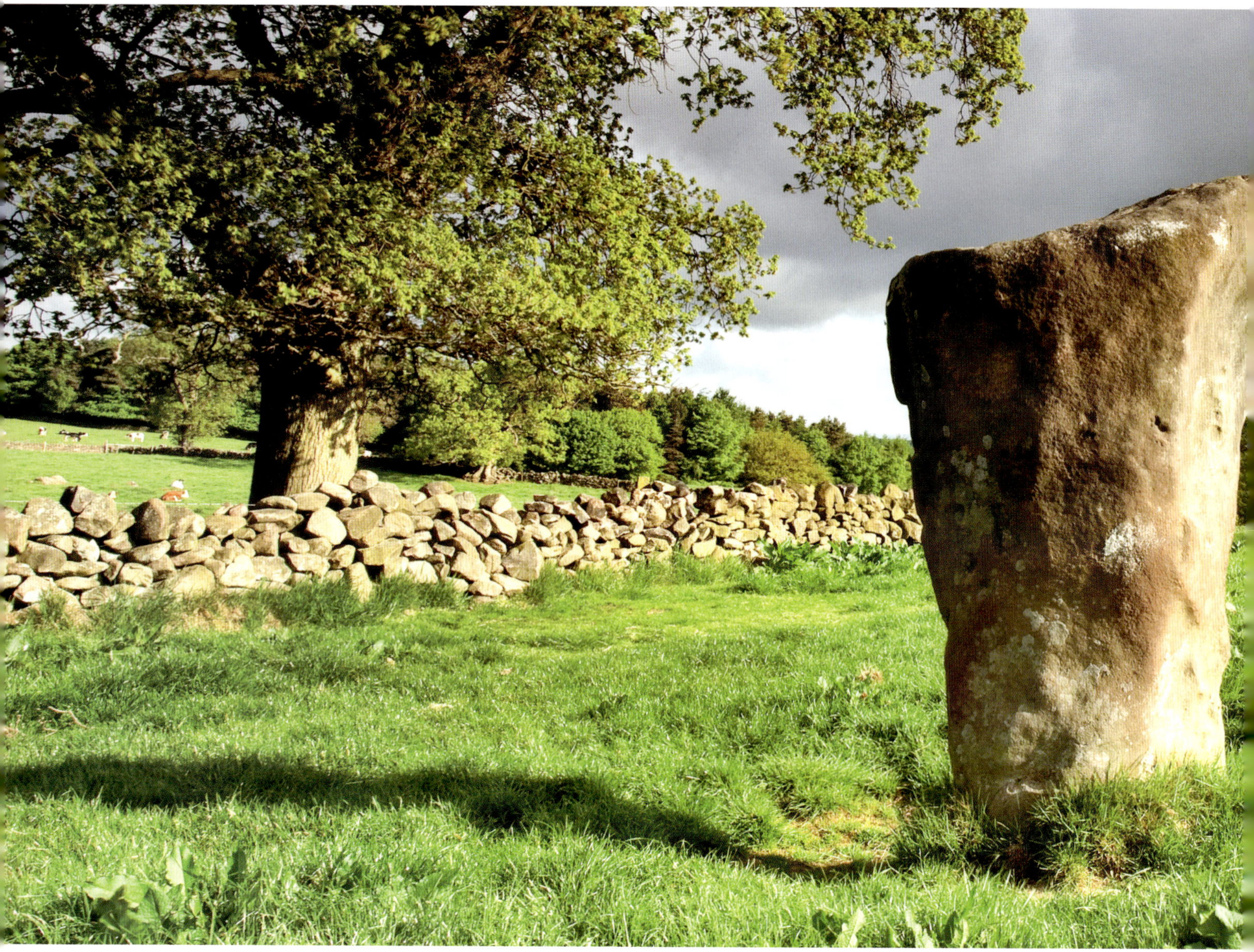

Nine Stone Close Stone Circle lies on Harthill Moor north of the village of Elton. There are now only four stones that remain with the tallest being 2.1 metres high making this the tallest stone circle in Derbyshire. Legend has it that the stones dance at midnight.

This leaning hawthorn tree was captured on a fine spring morning in the White Peak.

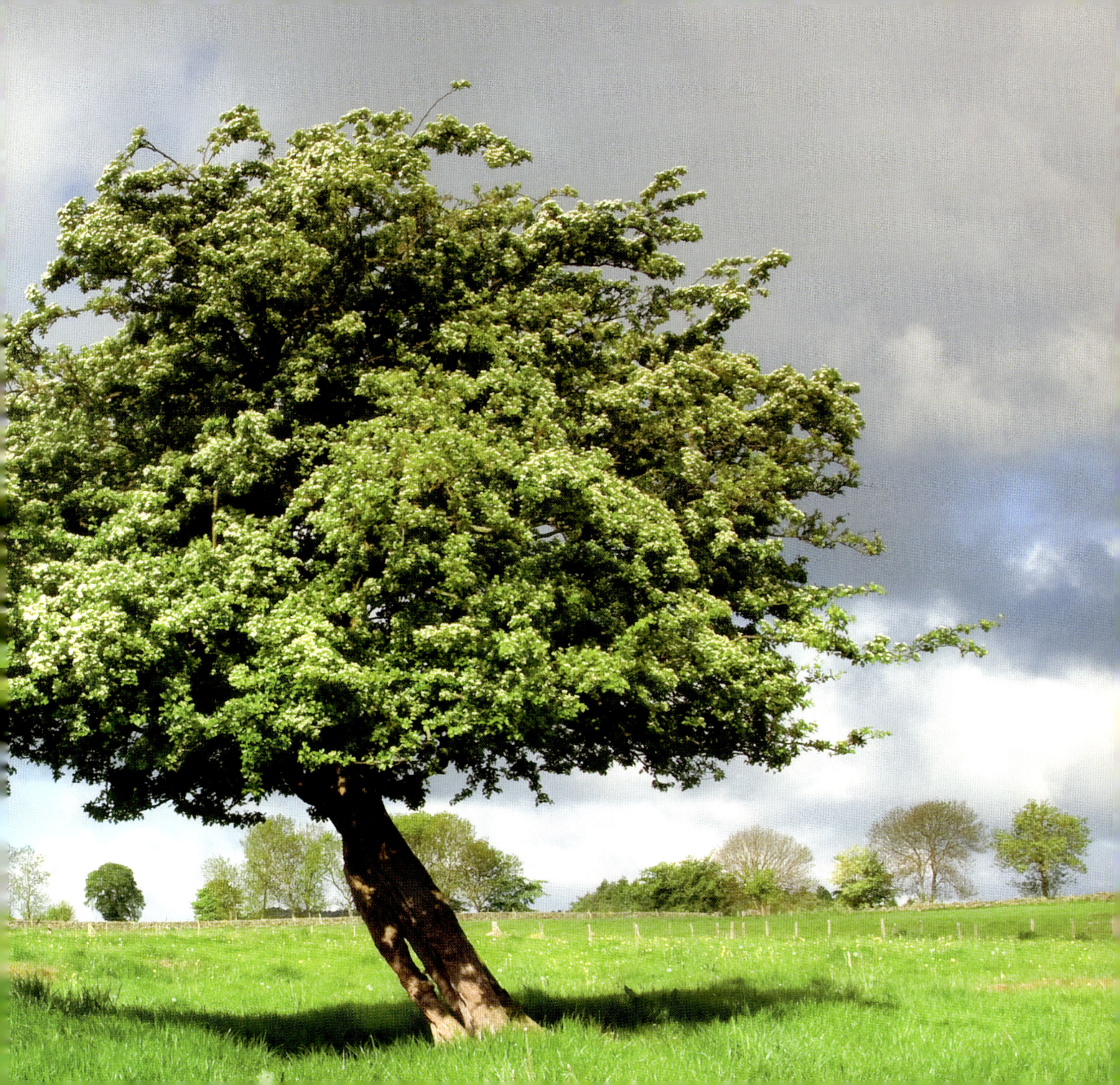

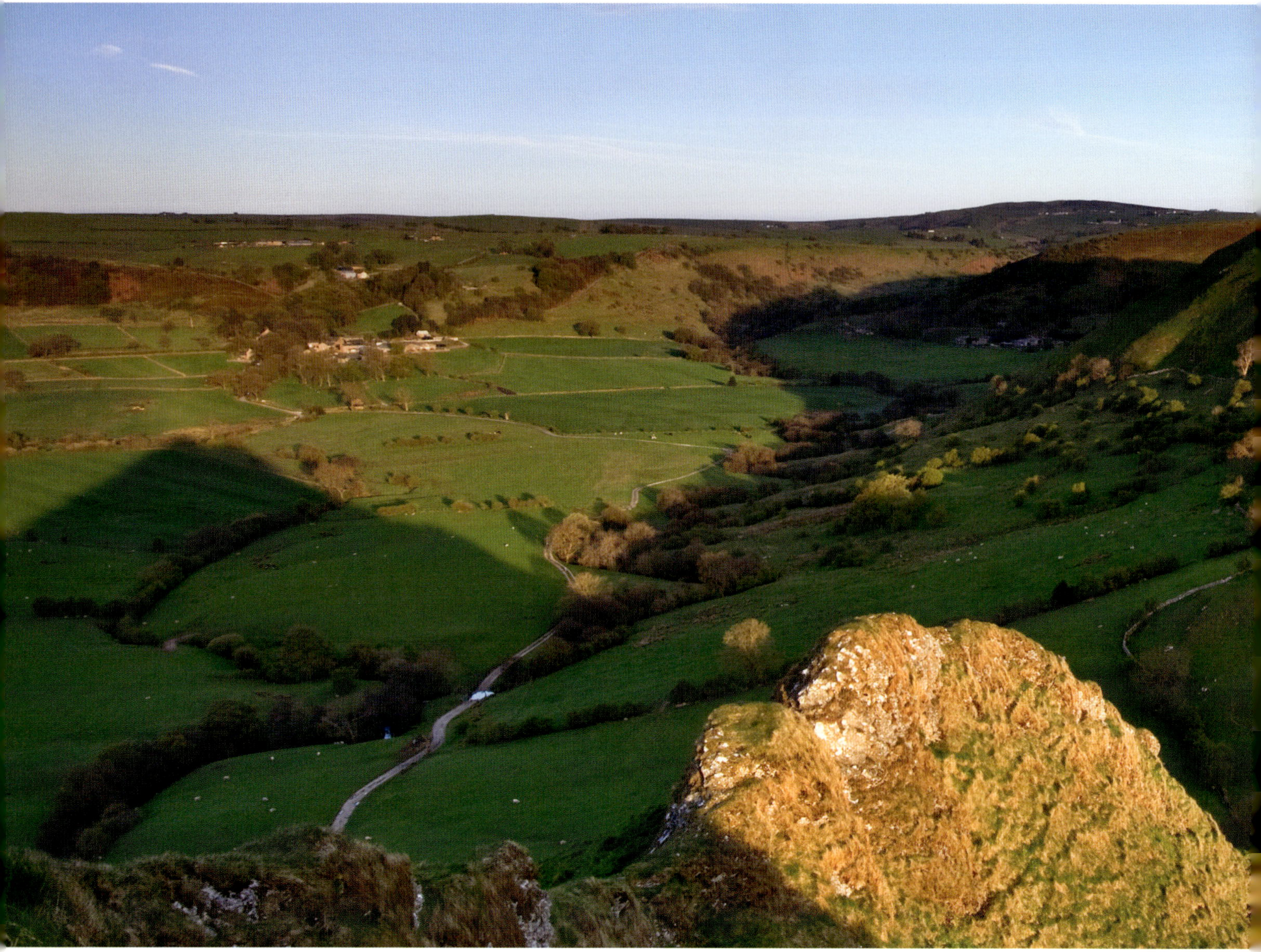

Although it can be a steep climb, the views from the top of Parkhouse Hill are absolutely stunning. Here Chrome Hill can be seen bathed by the early morning sunlight on a spring morning.

Leash Fen is an area of boggy moorland close to the village of Baslow. Here the cotton grass can be seen in flower at first light on a wonderfully clear morning.

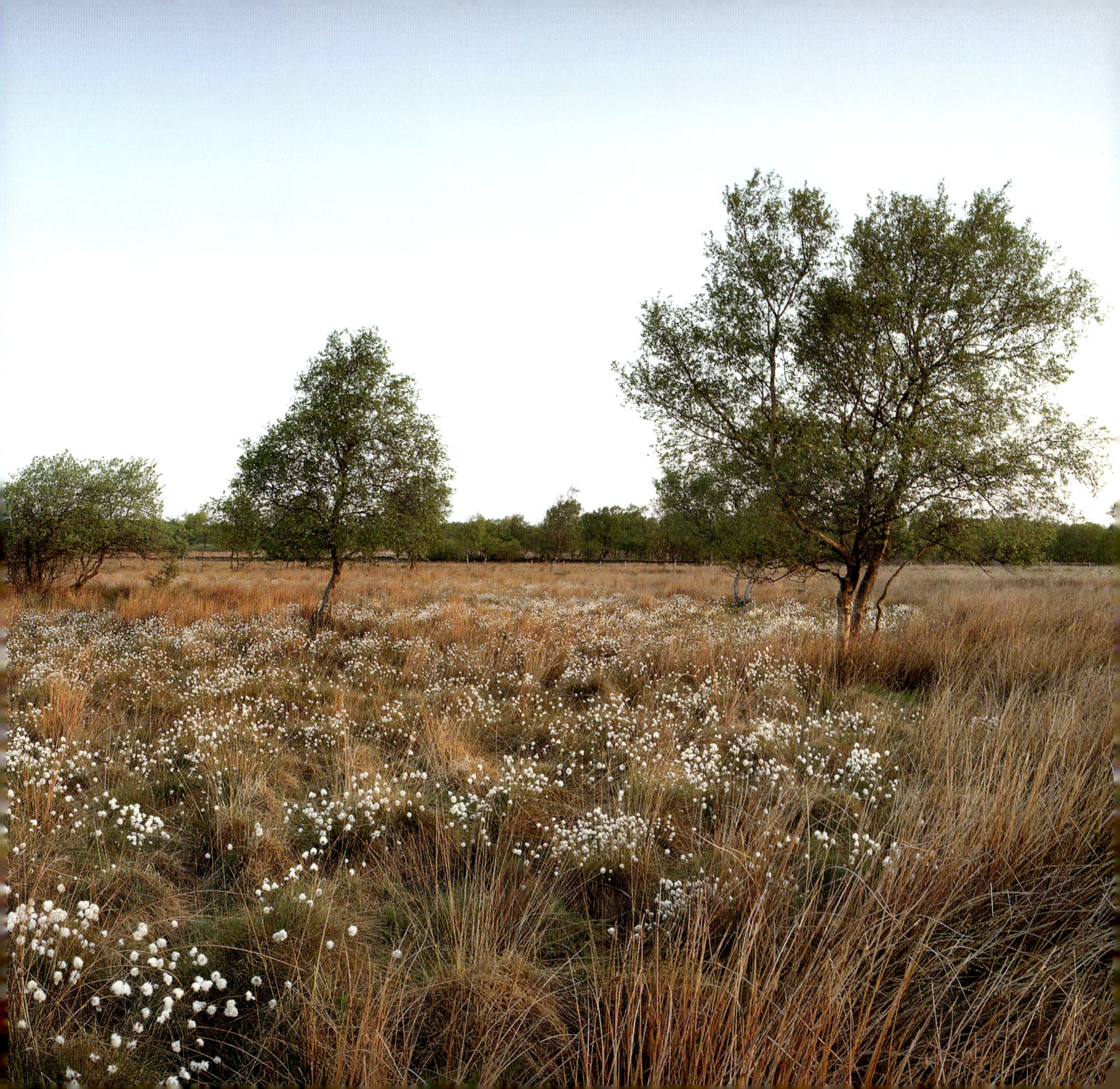

The first rays of the morning sun add warmth to this scene of St Anne's church in Baslow.

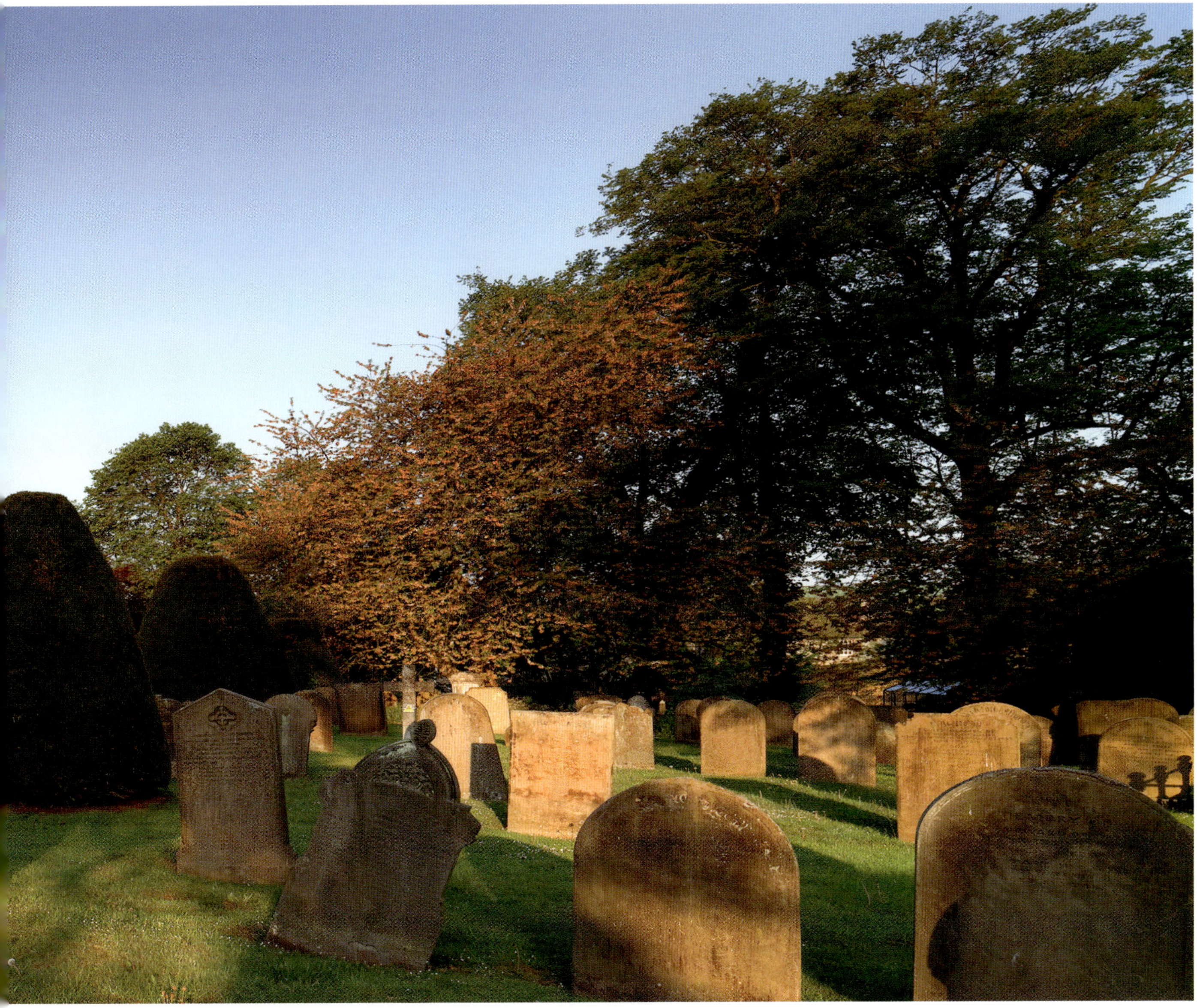

First light illuminates the rocks on Curbar Edge with spectacular cloud over the villages of Calver and Baslow in the distance.

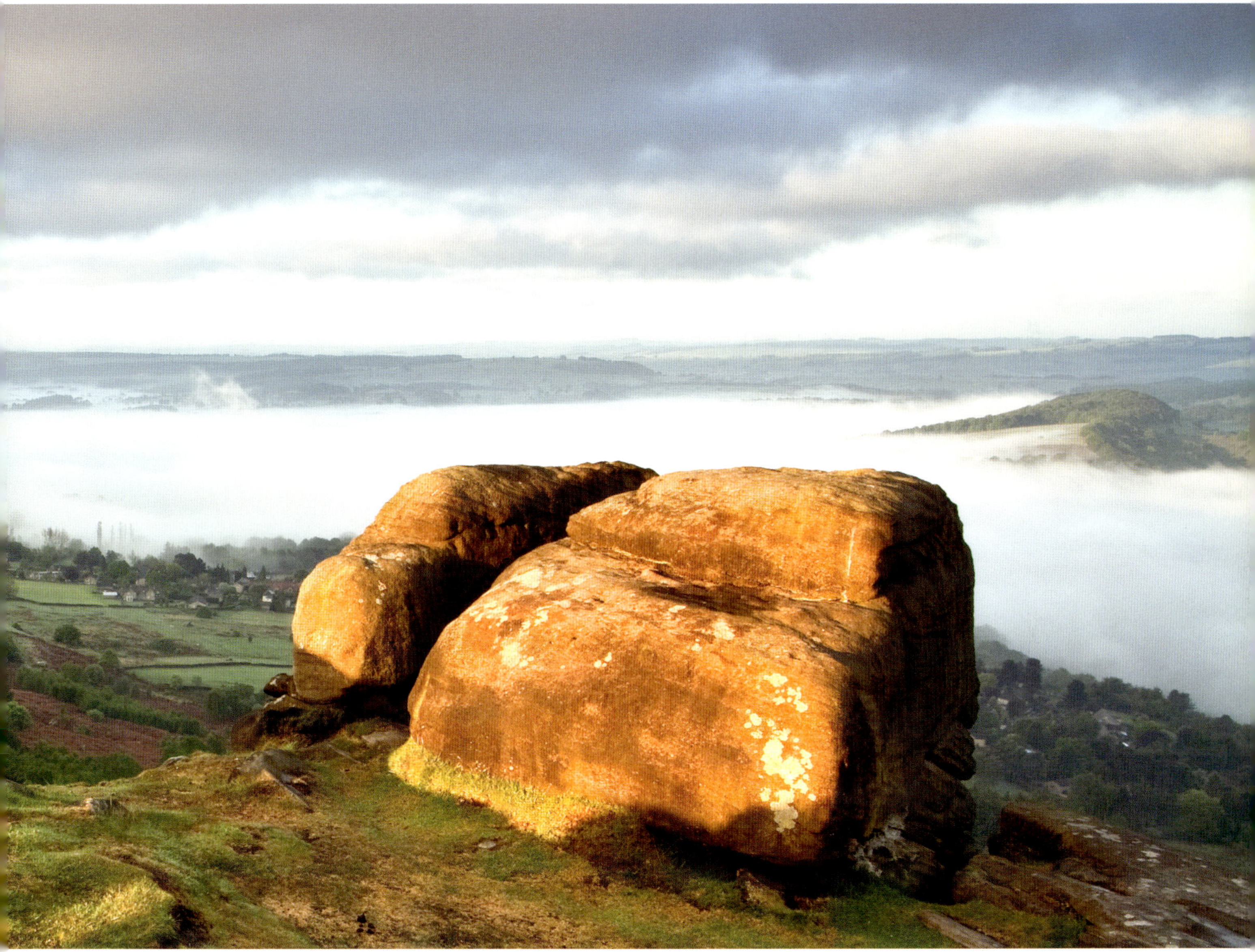

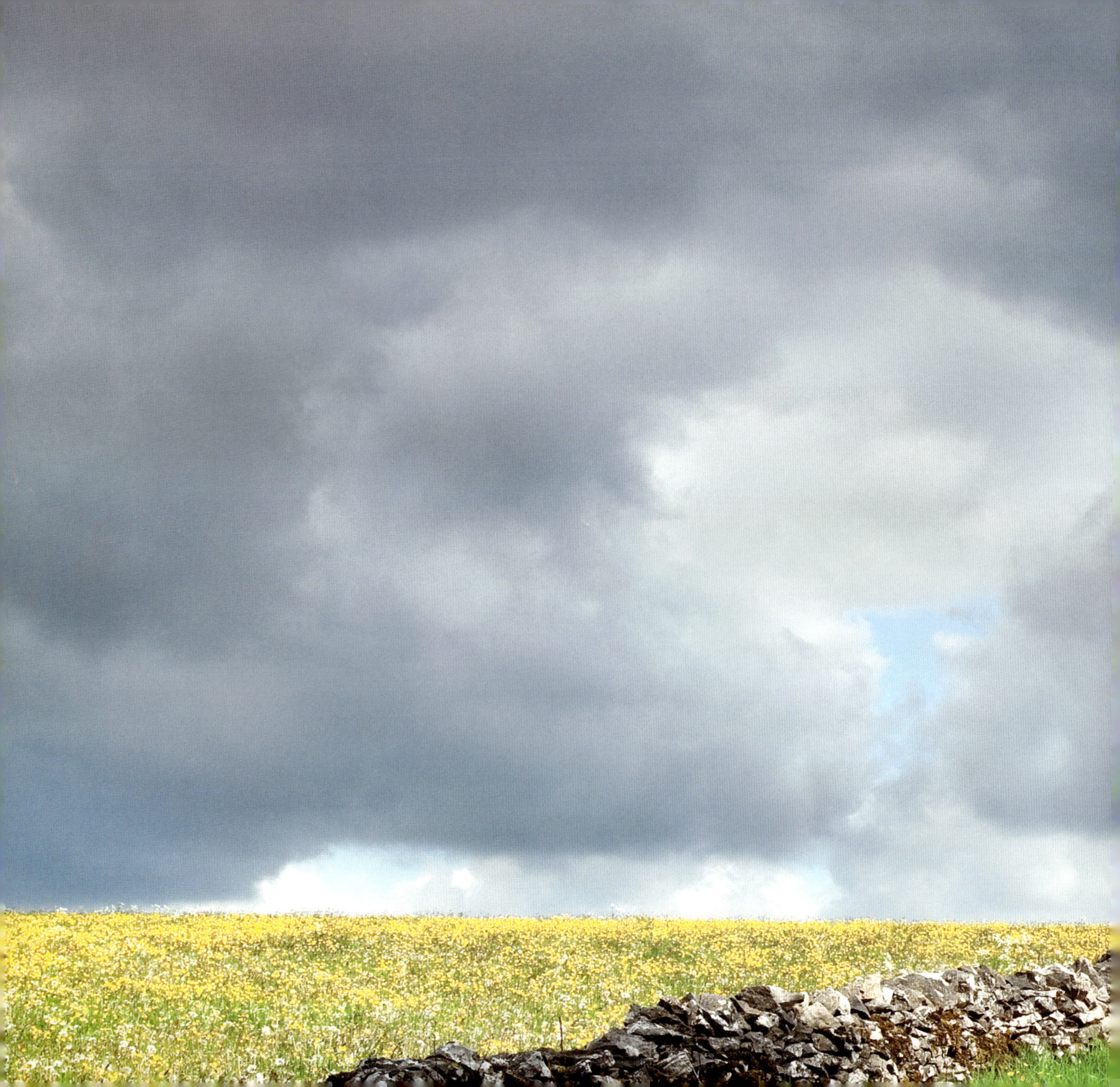

Storm clouds start to close in on this wonderful spring scene just outside the ancient village of Youlgreave.

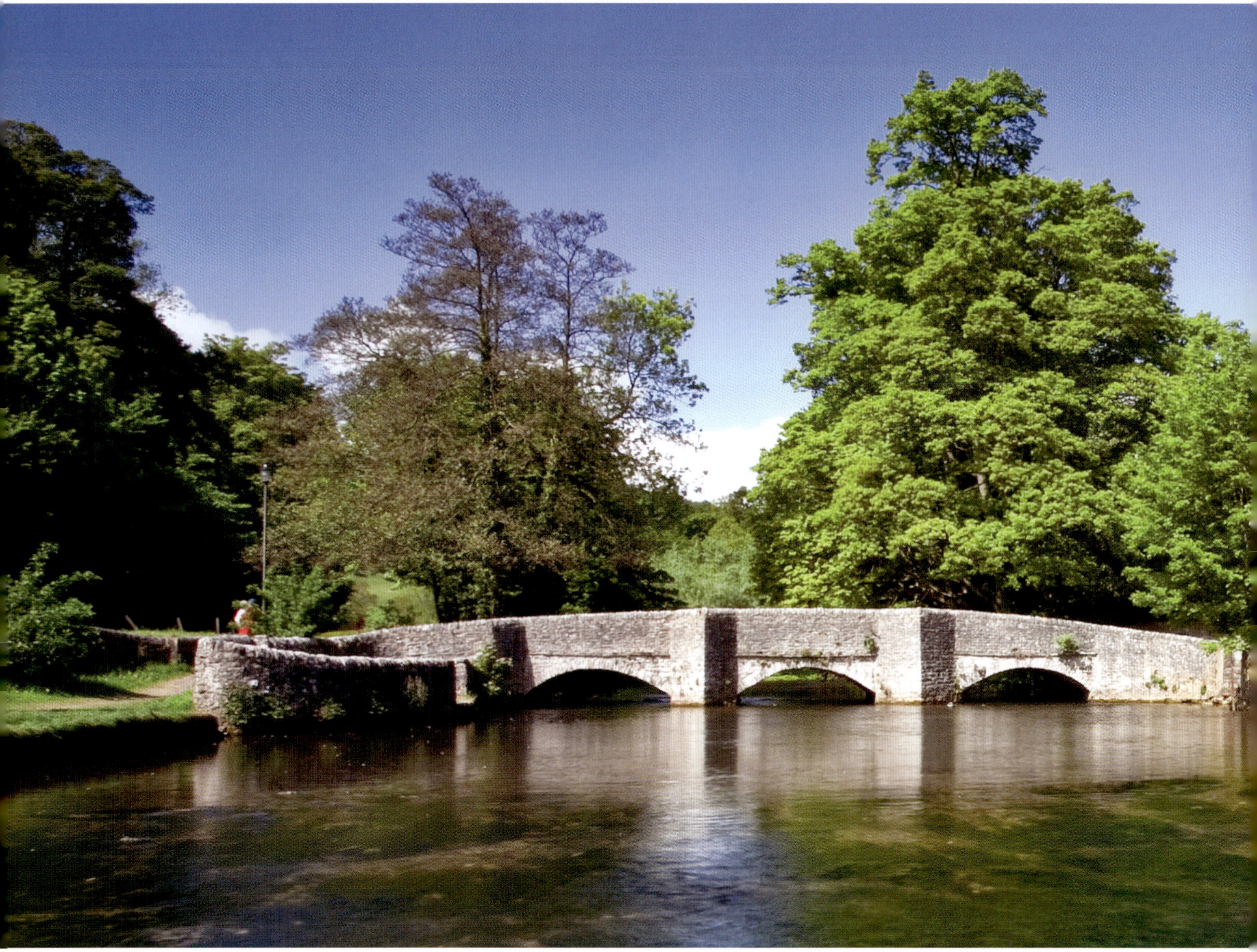

After driving past the famous medieval sheepwash bridge at Ashford in the Water and seeing the fantastic spring colours I couldn't resist stopping to grab a few quick images. Luckily I had some wellington boots in the car and was able to head out into the middle of the River Wye for a better viewpoint.

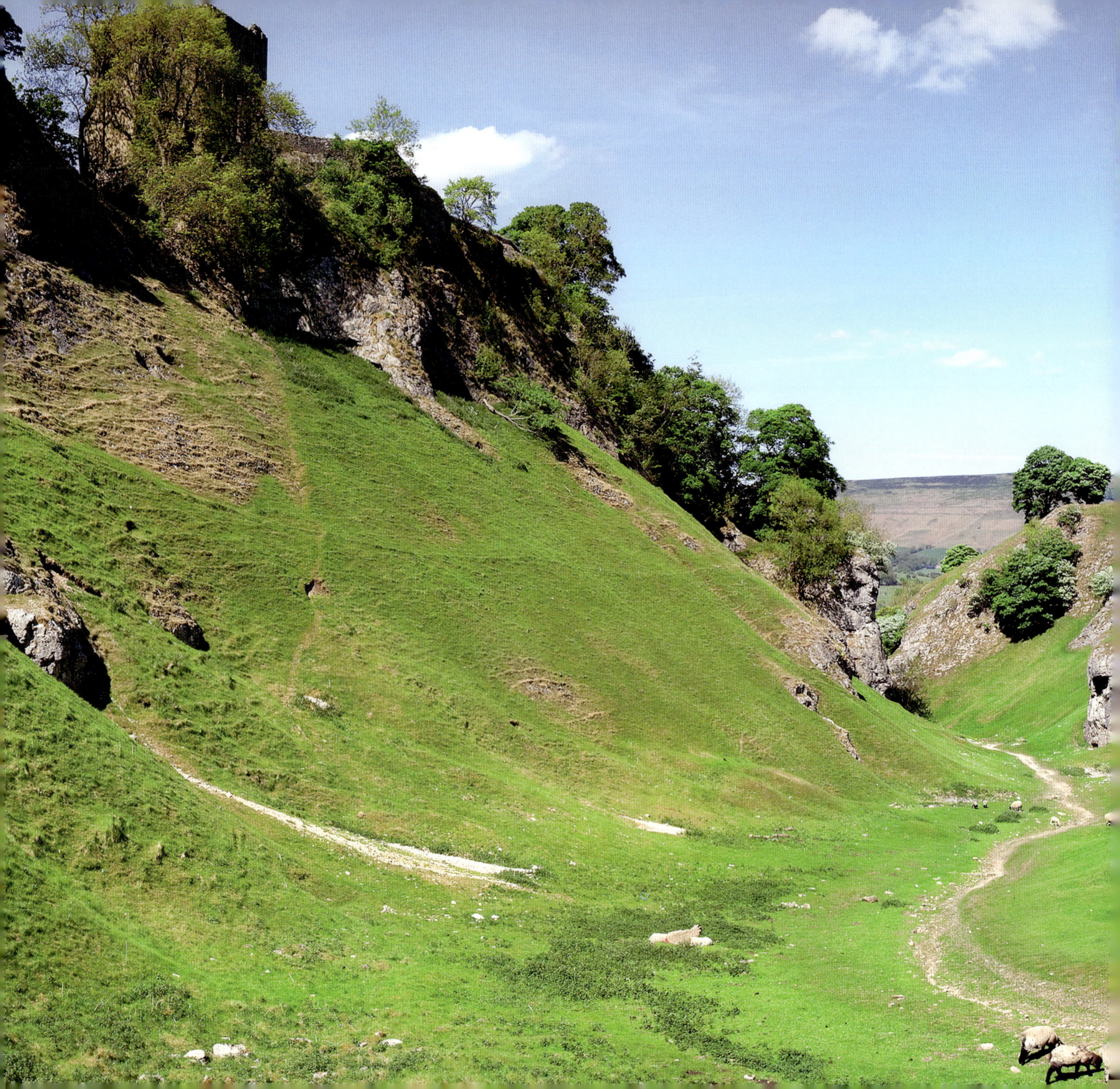

The winding footpath snaking through the limestone valley of Cave Dale towards the village of Castleton.

Peveril Castle stands high on a cliff top above the village of Castleton providing excellent views of Cave Dale and the Hope Valley. The castle is named after William Peveril who was granted Royal Manors of the Peak shortly after the Norman conquest in 1066. Peveril created the village of Castleton and around 1080 he fortified the site of the present castle and constructed a wooden keep which was later replaced with stone.

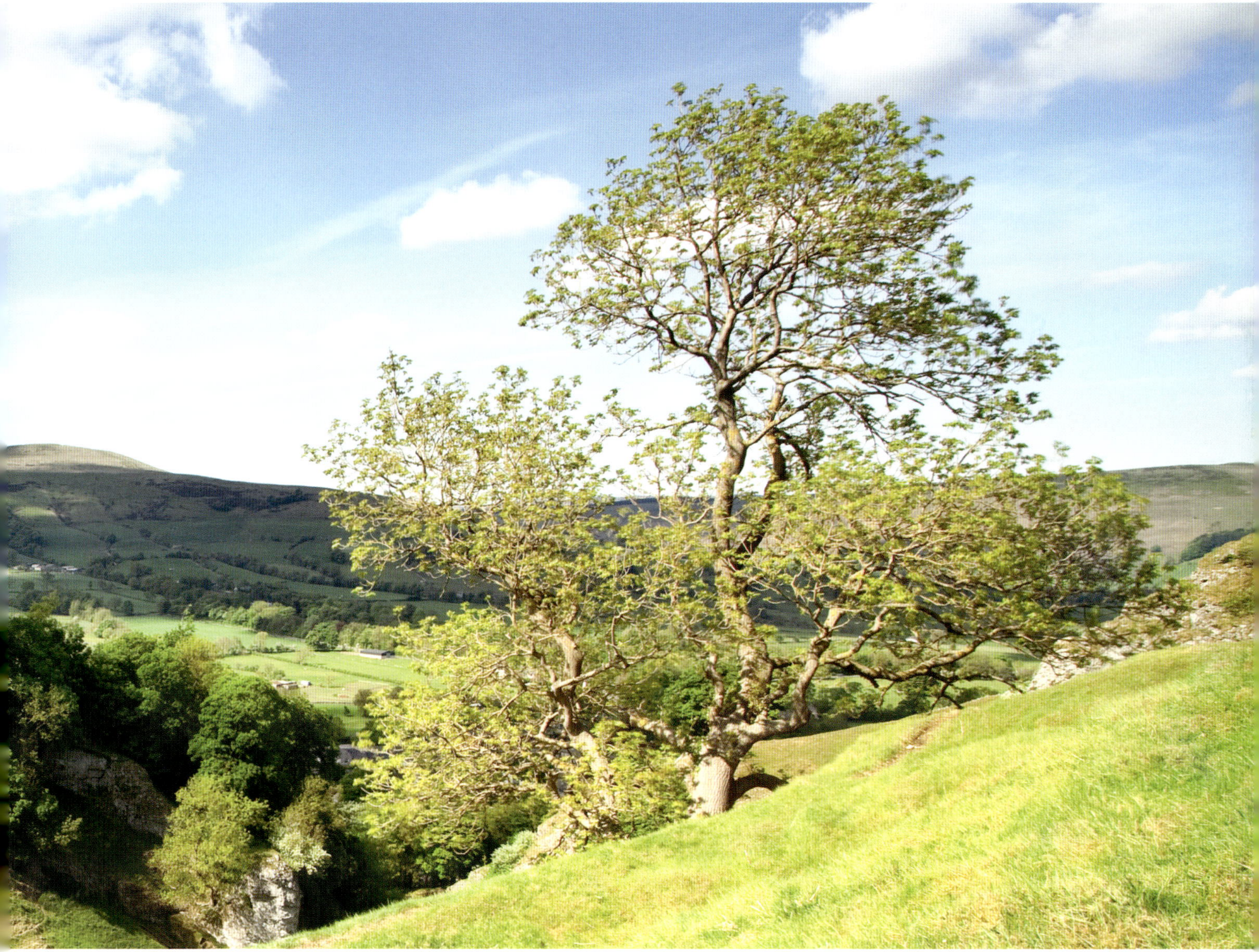

Morning mist covers the surrounding countryside beneath Baslow Edge on a cold spring morning.

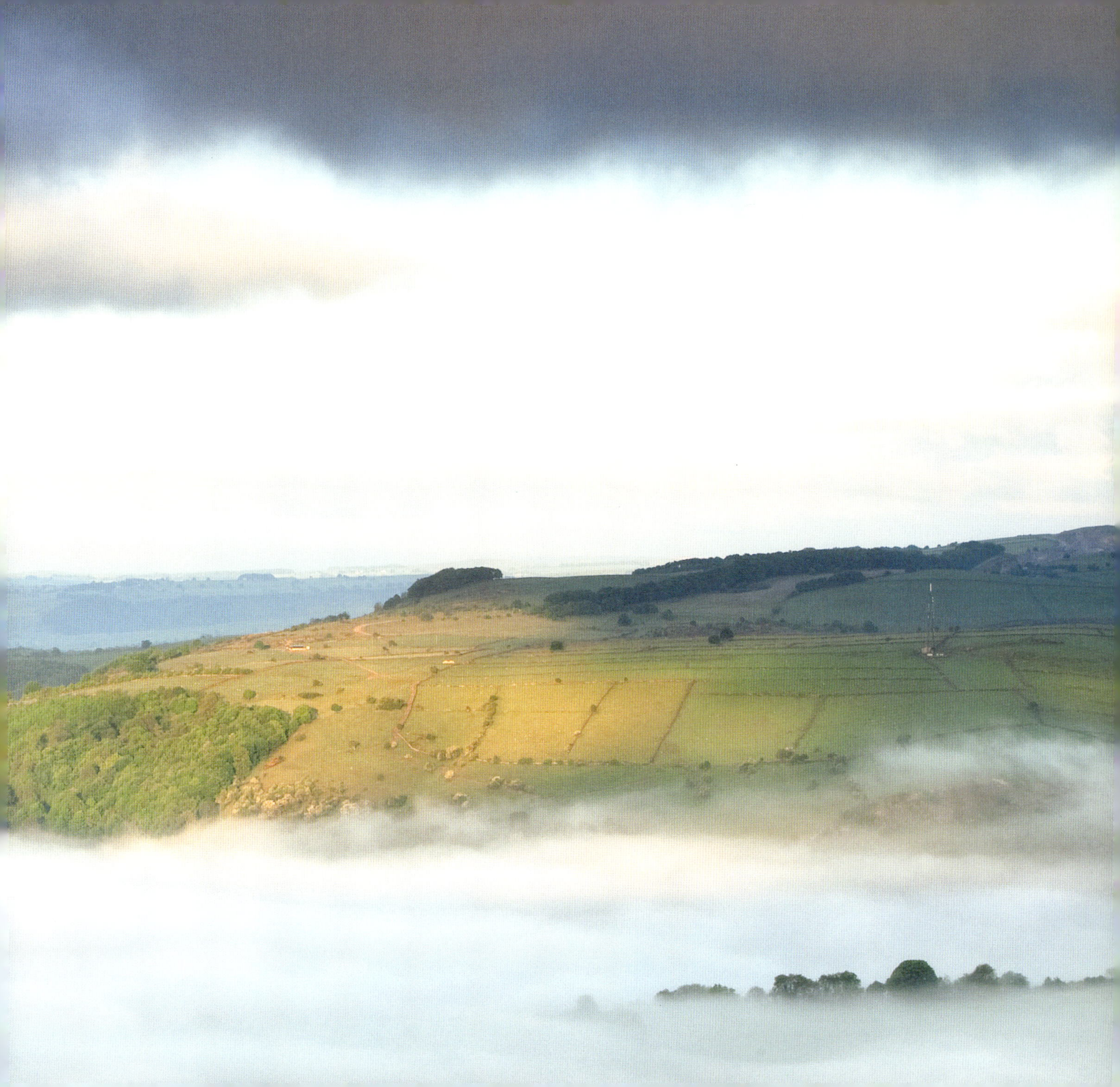

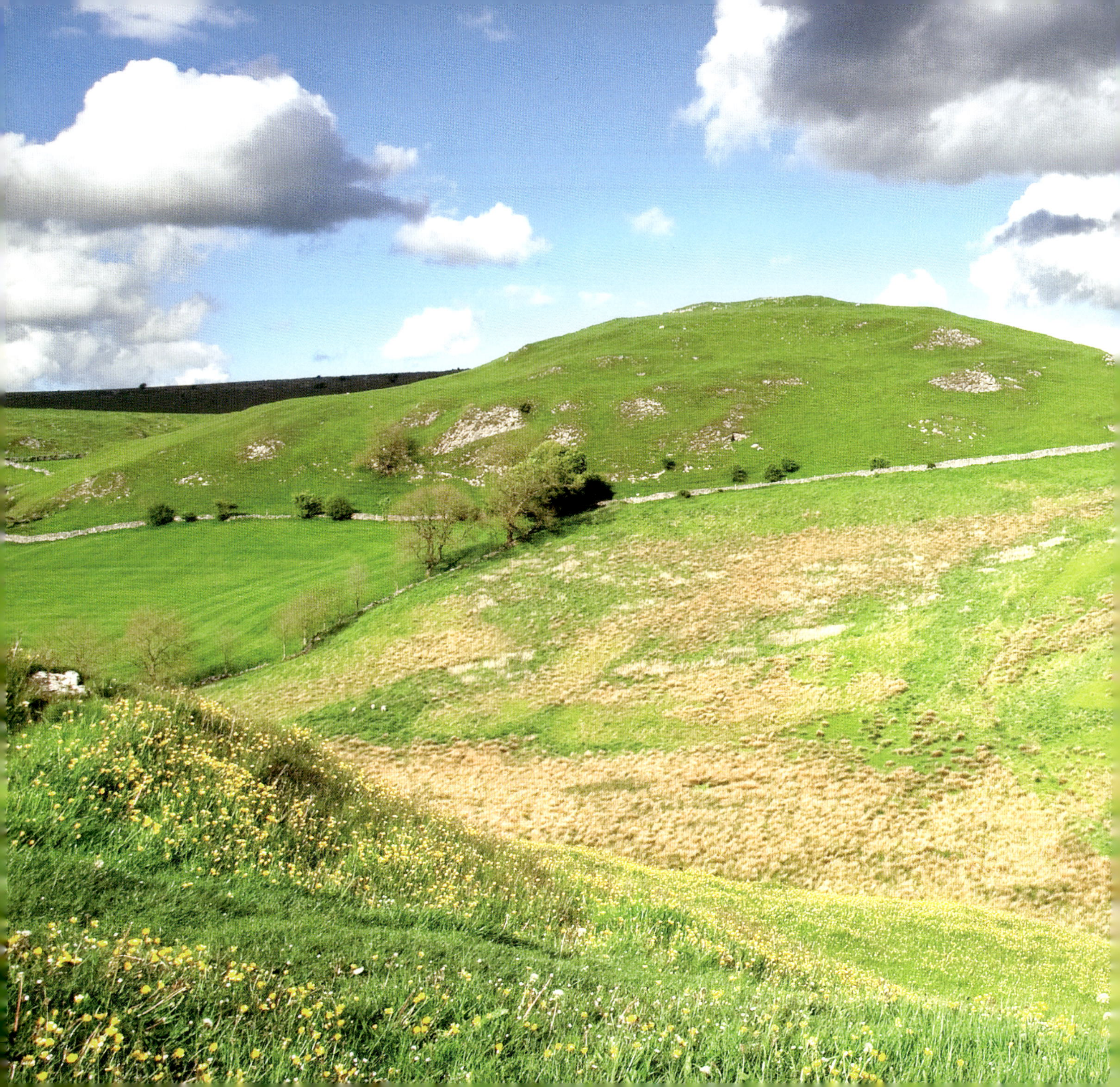

Buttercups adorning the slopes of Chrome Hill with the distinctive Parkhouse Hill to the right, also known as the Dragons Back due to its unique shape.

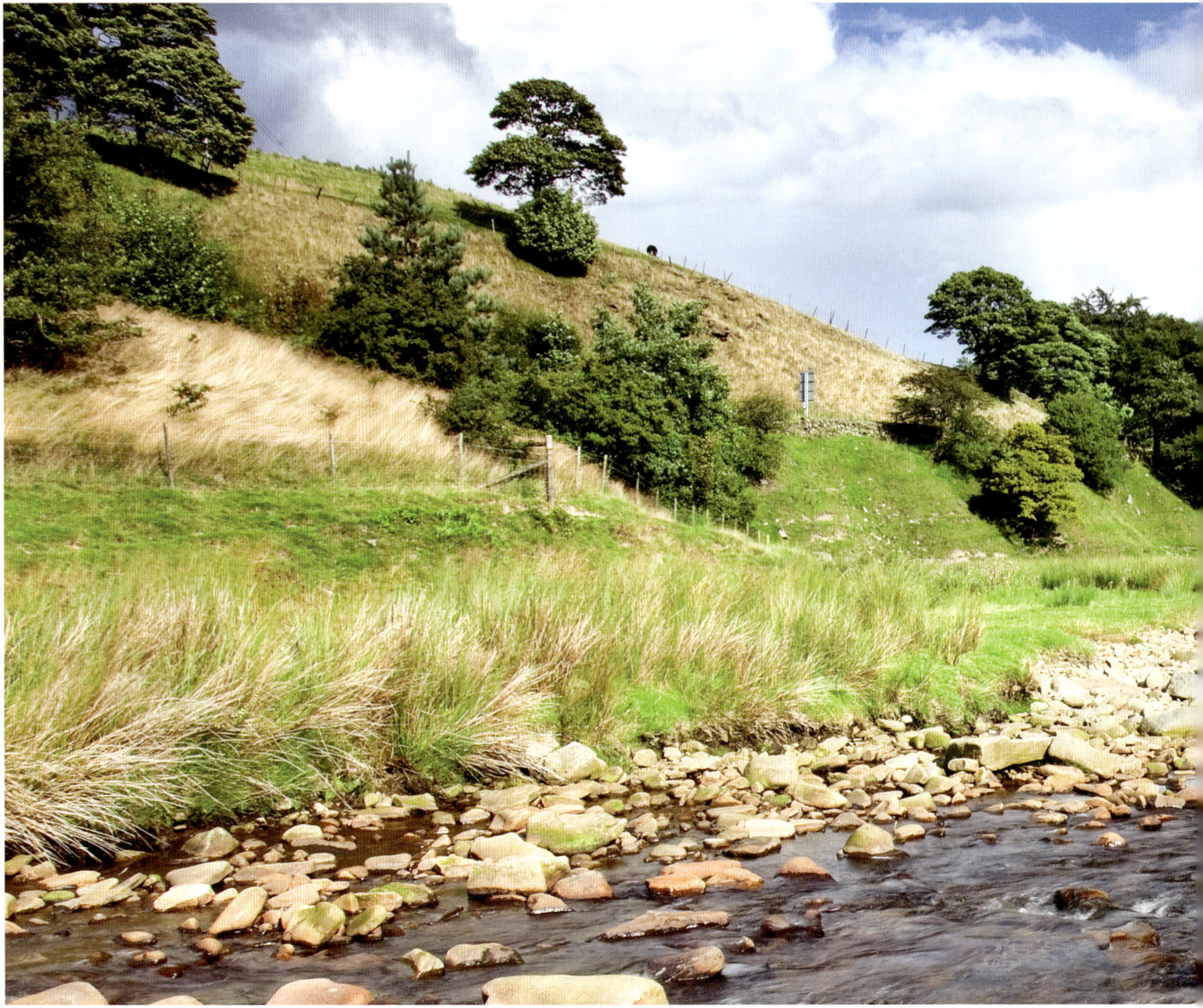

The River Ashop flows approximately ten miles from its source on Black Ashop Moor before passing through the valley in this image and then finally emptying into Ladybower Reservoir.

As the summer sun starts to rise above the horizon these rocks on Higger Tor are suffused with warmth with the flowering heather in the foreground adding a further splash of summer colour.

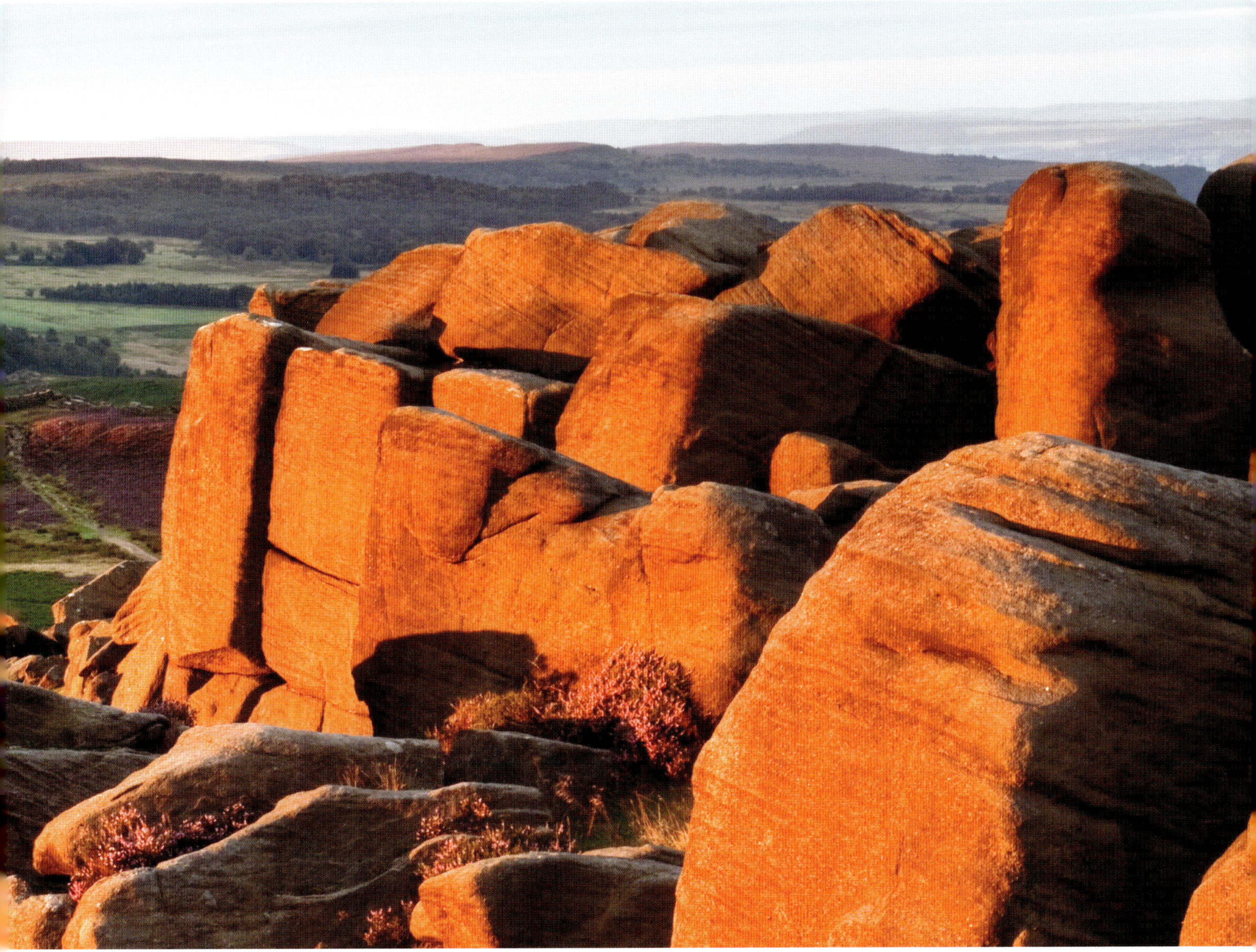

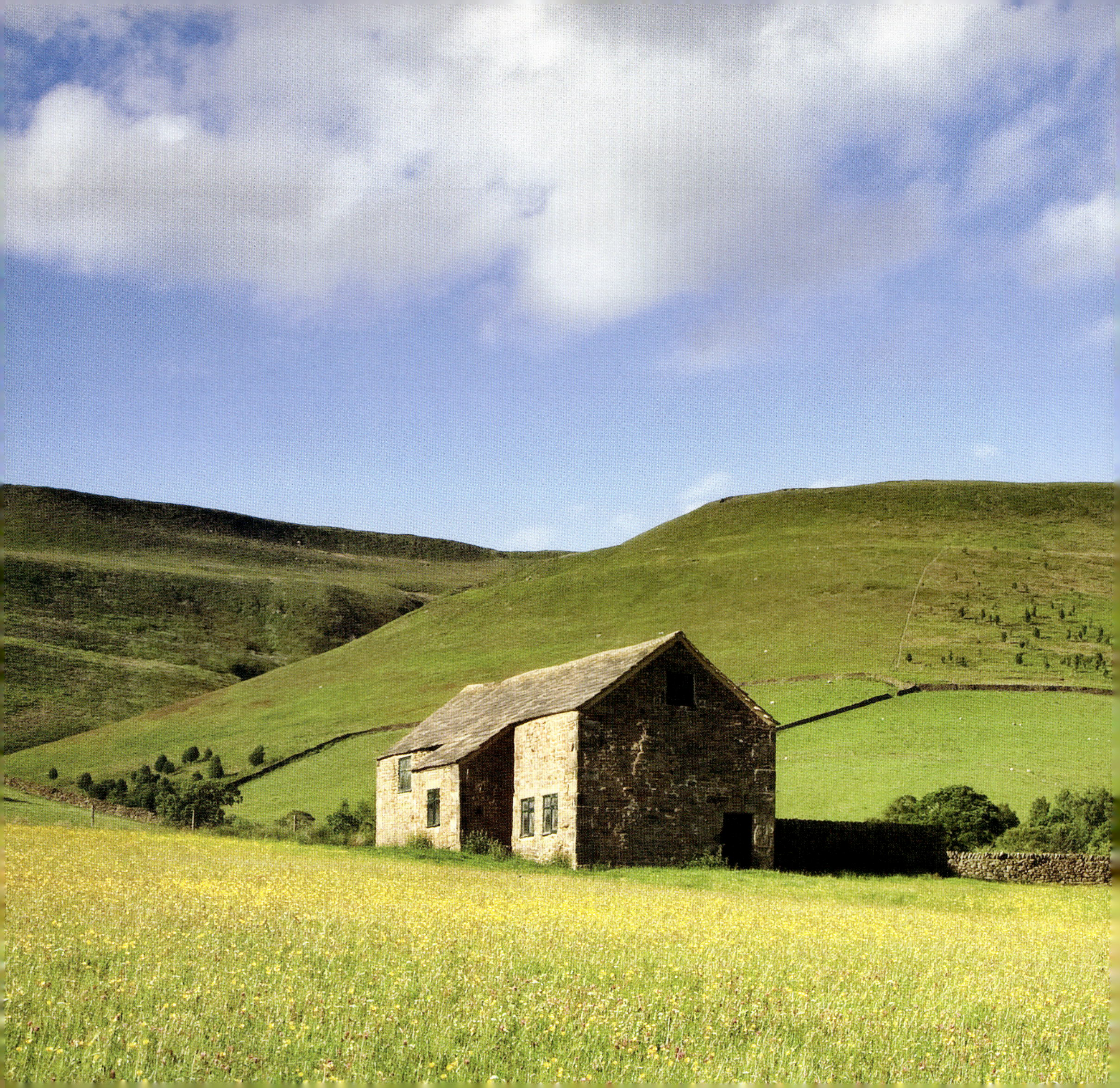

A picturesque stone barn captured on a summer's evening at Upper Booth on the way up to Kinder Scout.

Looking up towards the dominant rocky ridge of the Roaches with the summer heather in full bloom on a lovely calm evening in Staffordshire.

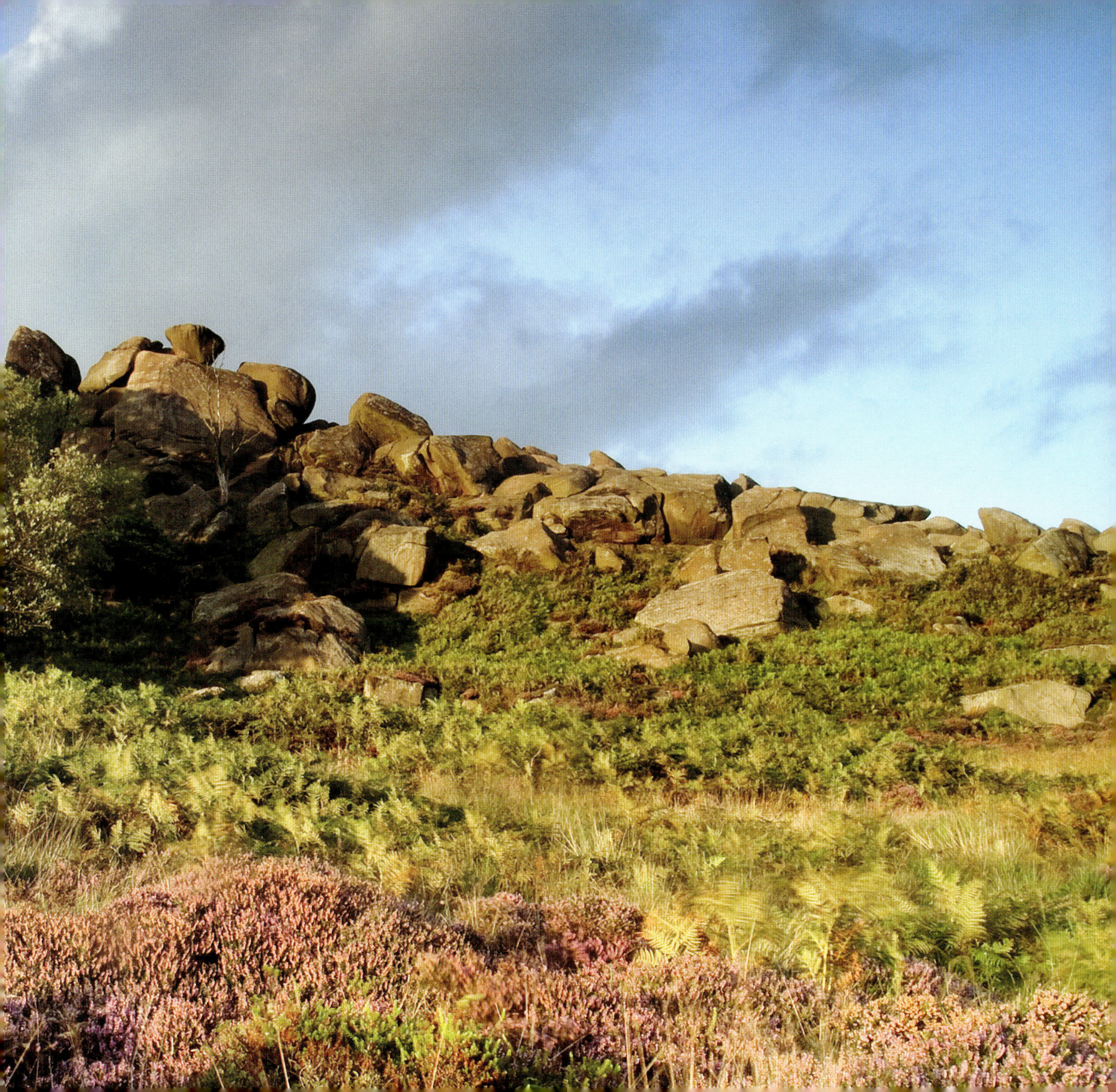

Mother Cap sits on Owler Moor and is one of the Peak District's most distinctive outcrops. The rock can be seen for miles around and theories suggest that it may once have been used as a marker and could have been illuminated by fire at night. Here it can be seen lit by the first rays of the sun on a fine August morning.

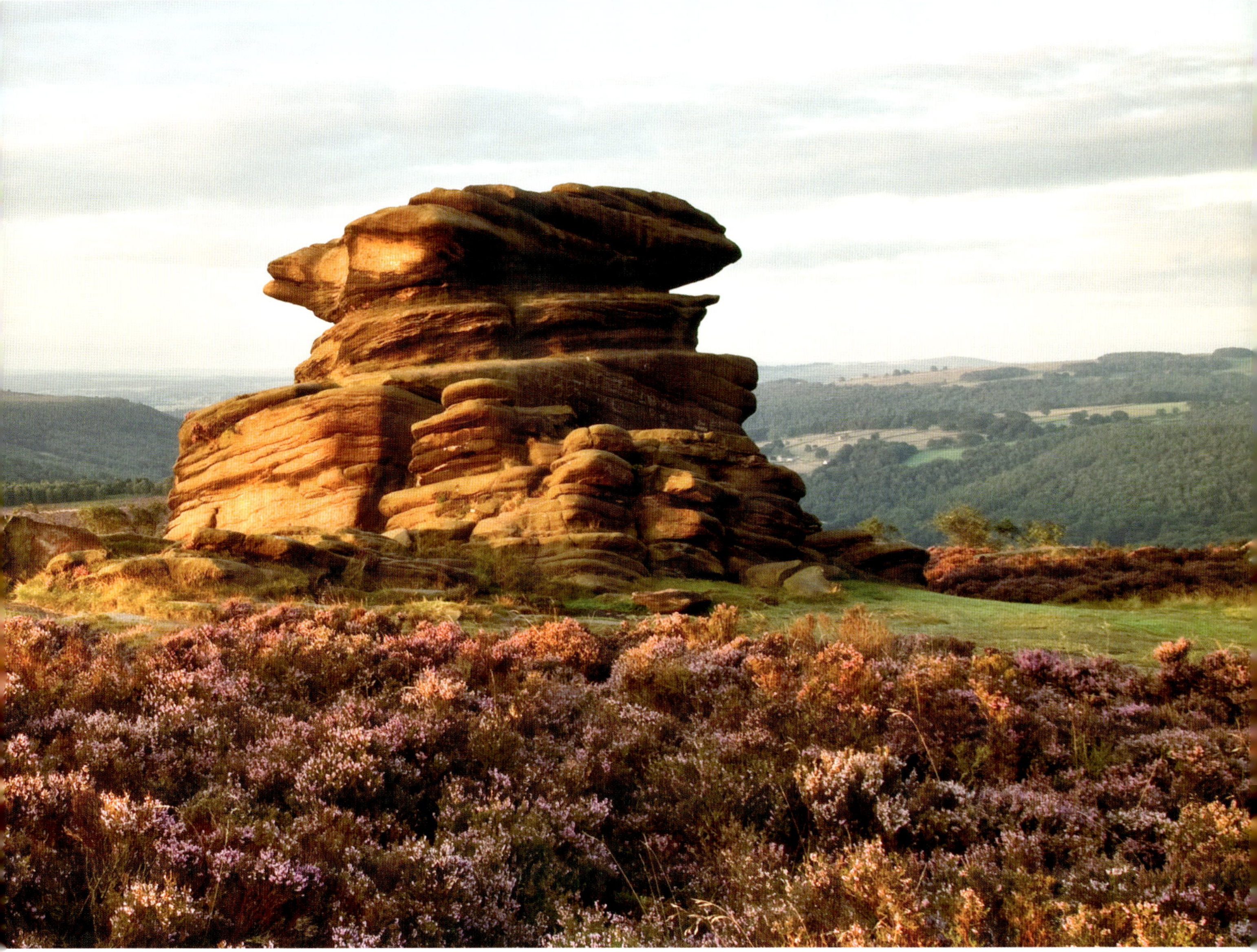

Morning light on the gritstone outcrop of Over Owler Tor, with the Hope Valley visible in the distance.

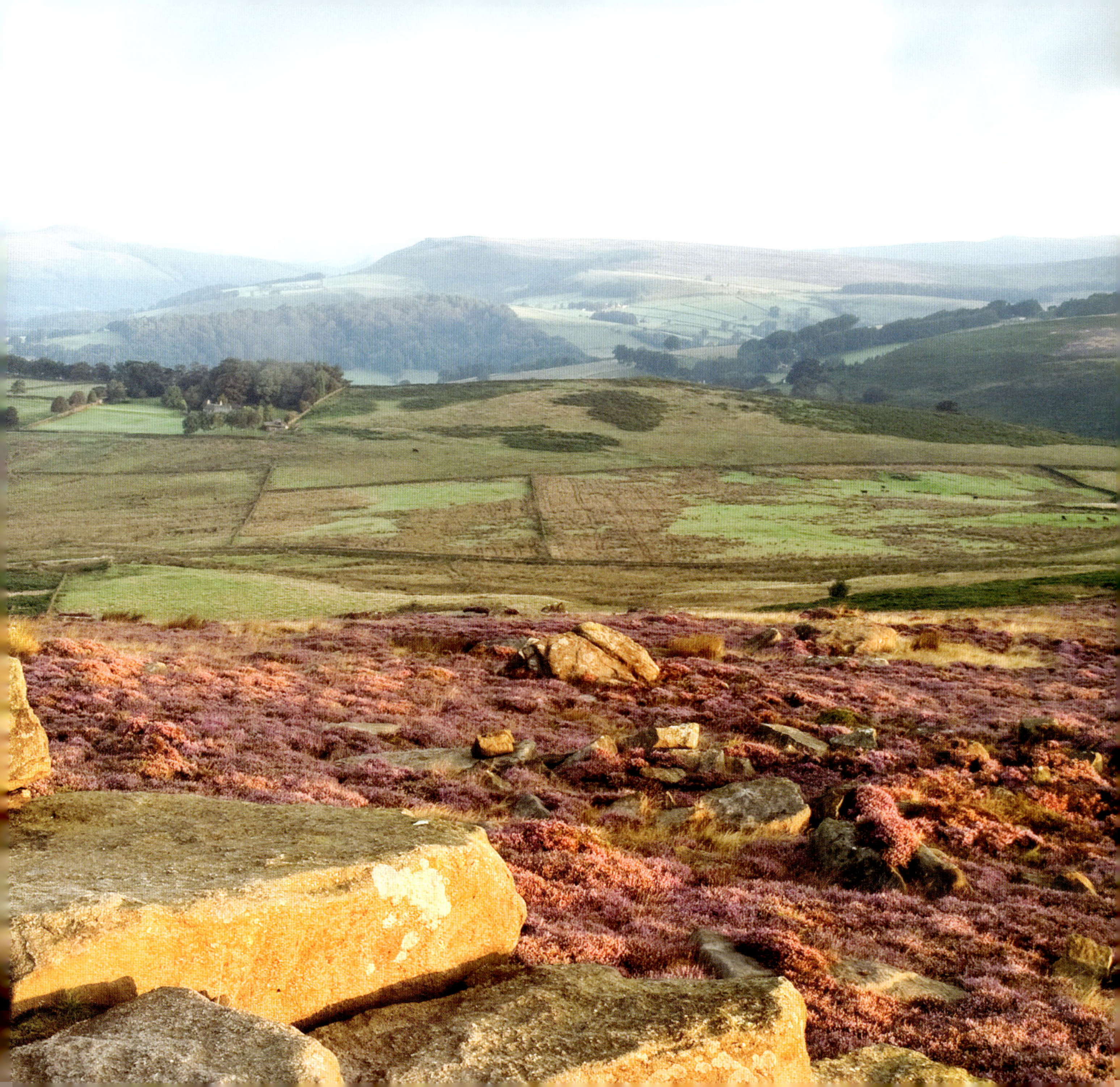

Shafts of light start to break through the cloudy sky and illuminate the countryside around Curbar Edge.

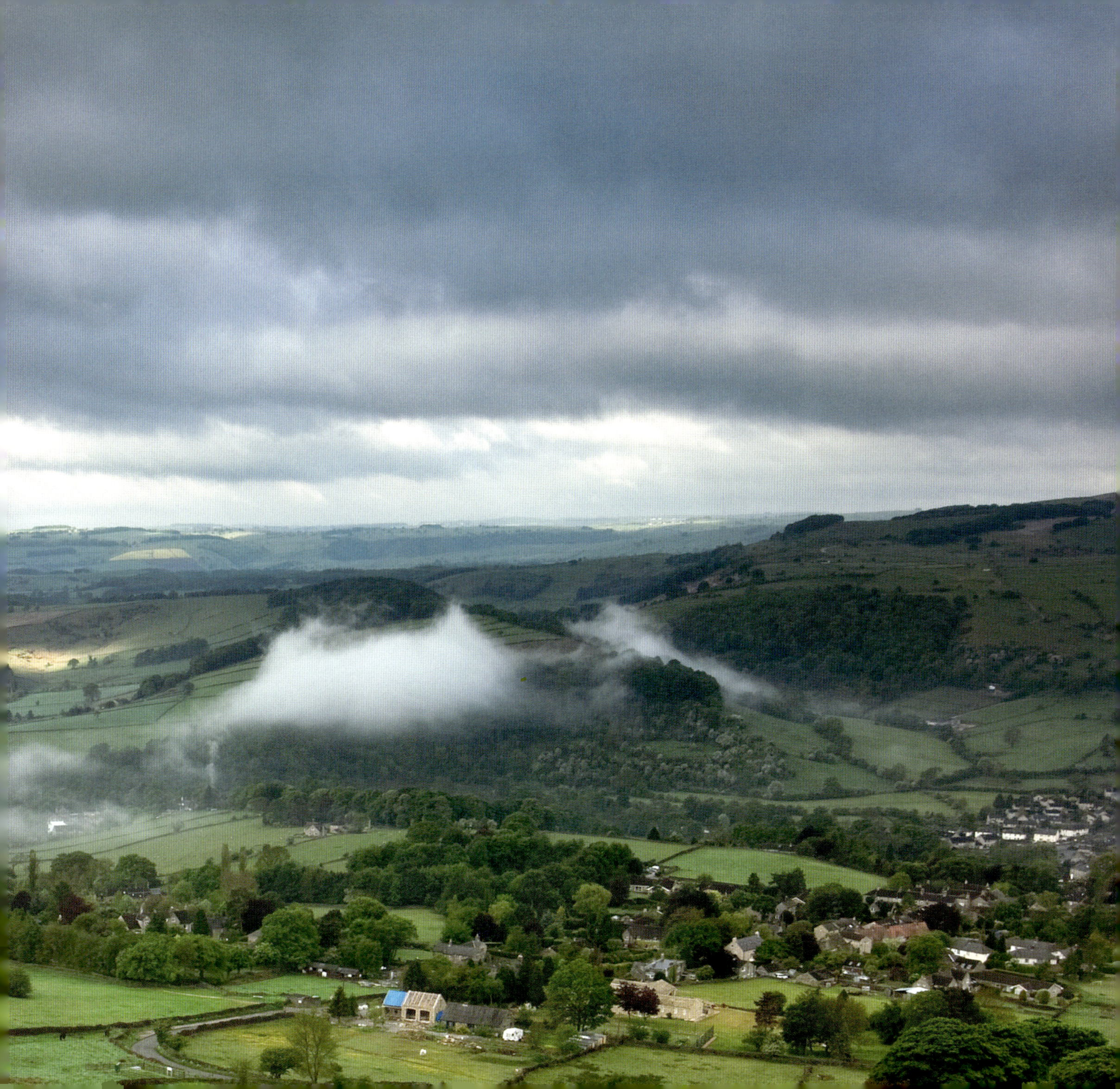

Dawn light illuminating the heather and rocks on top of Stanage Edge.

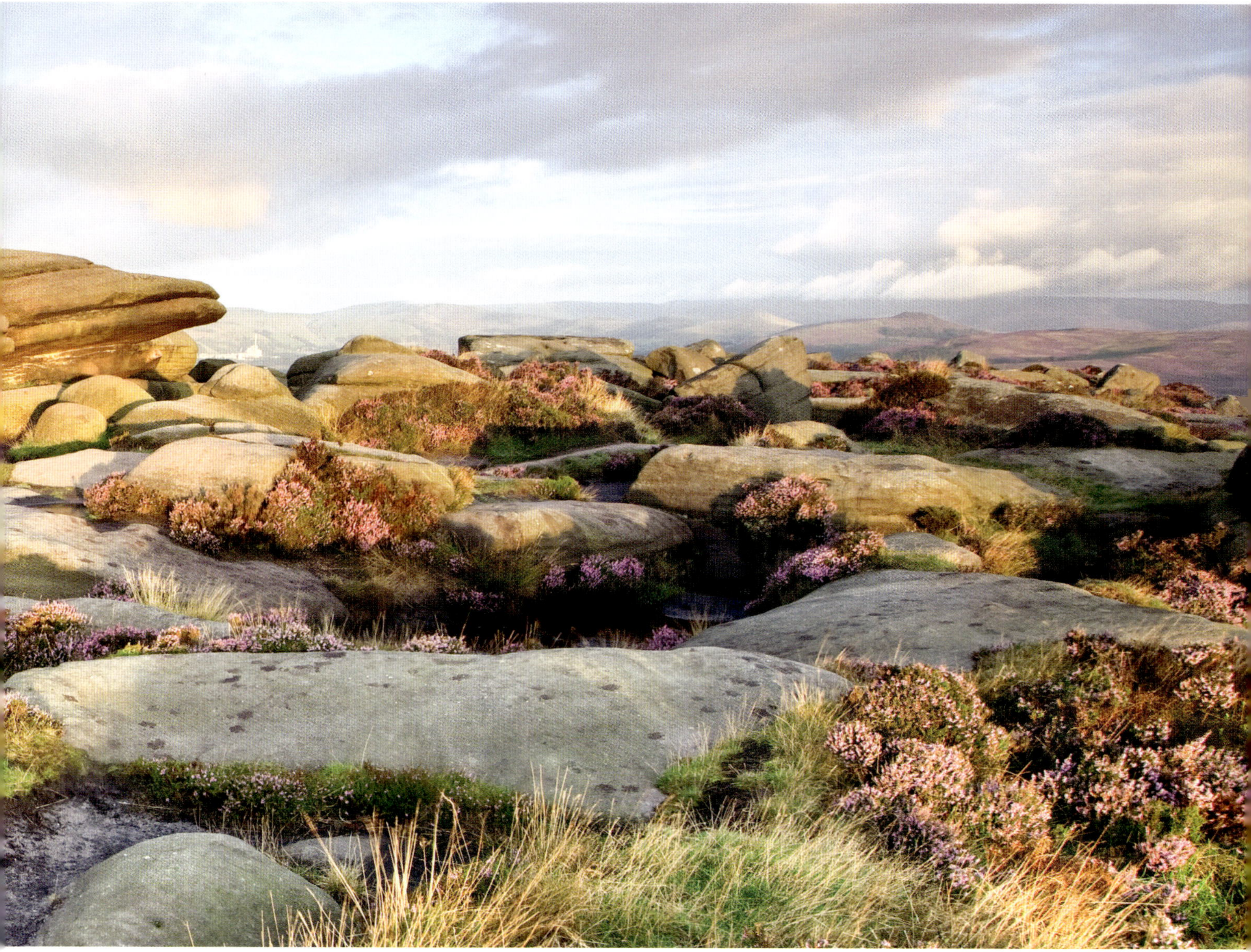

Centuries of wind and rain have chiselled out interesting shapes on many rocky outcrops in the Peak District. This boulder on top of Carhead Rocks is often referred to as the Knuckle Stone. The view from Carhead Rocks looking towards the Hope Valley is one of the finest in the Peak District.

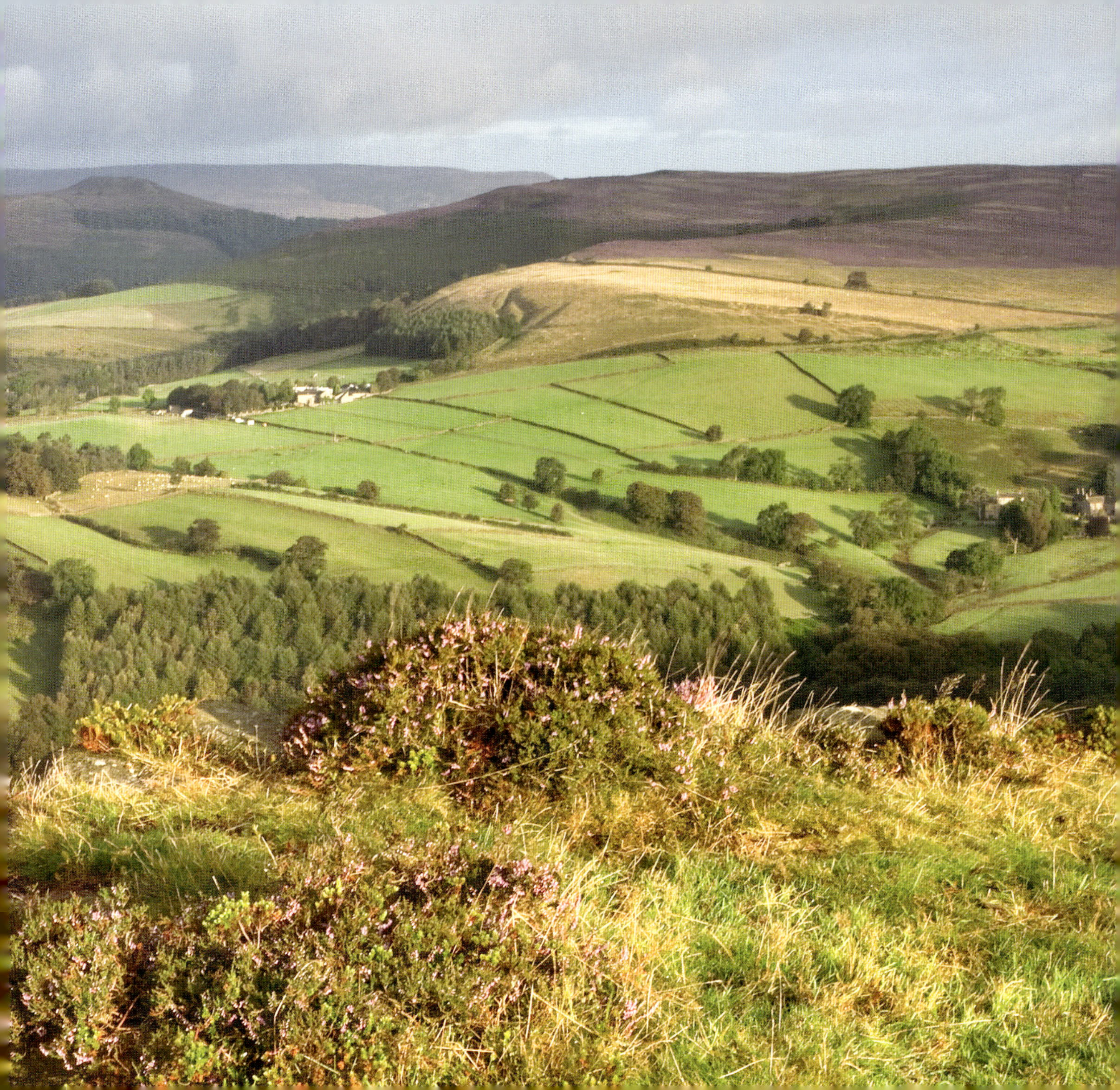

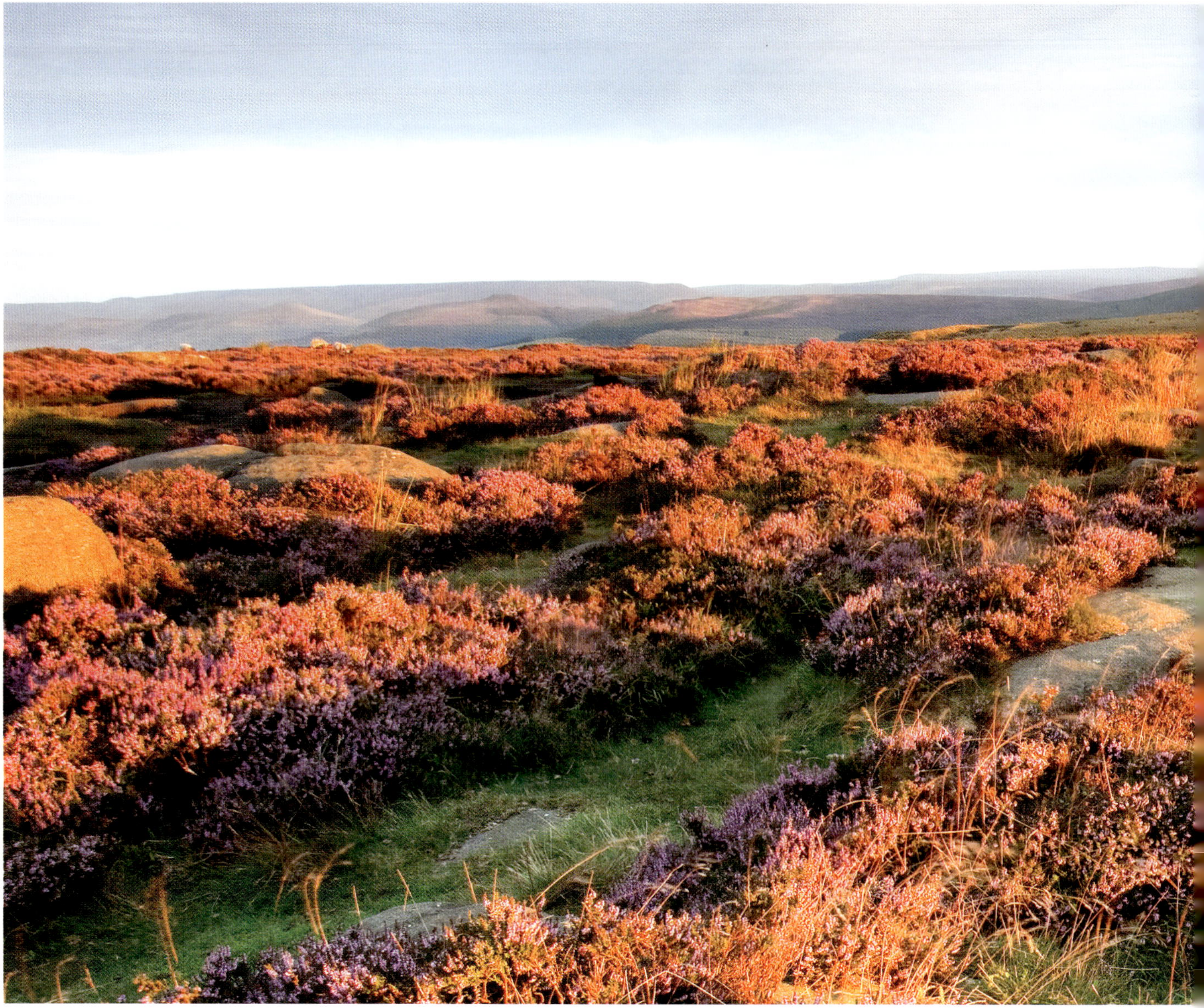

Beautiful dawn summer light catches the rocks and heather on Burbage Edge on an August morning in the Peak District.

Late evening sunshine adds a fantastic warm glow to the rocks and brings out the best of the colour in the flowering heather on Carhead Rocks.

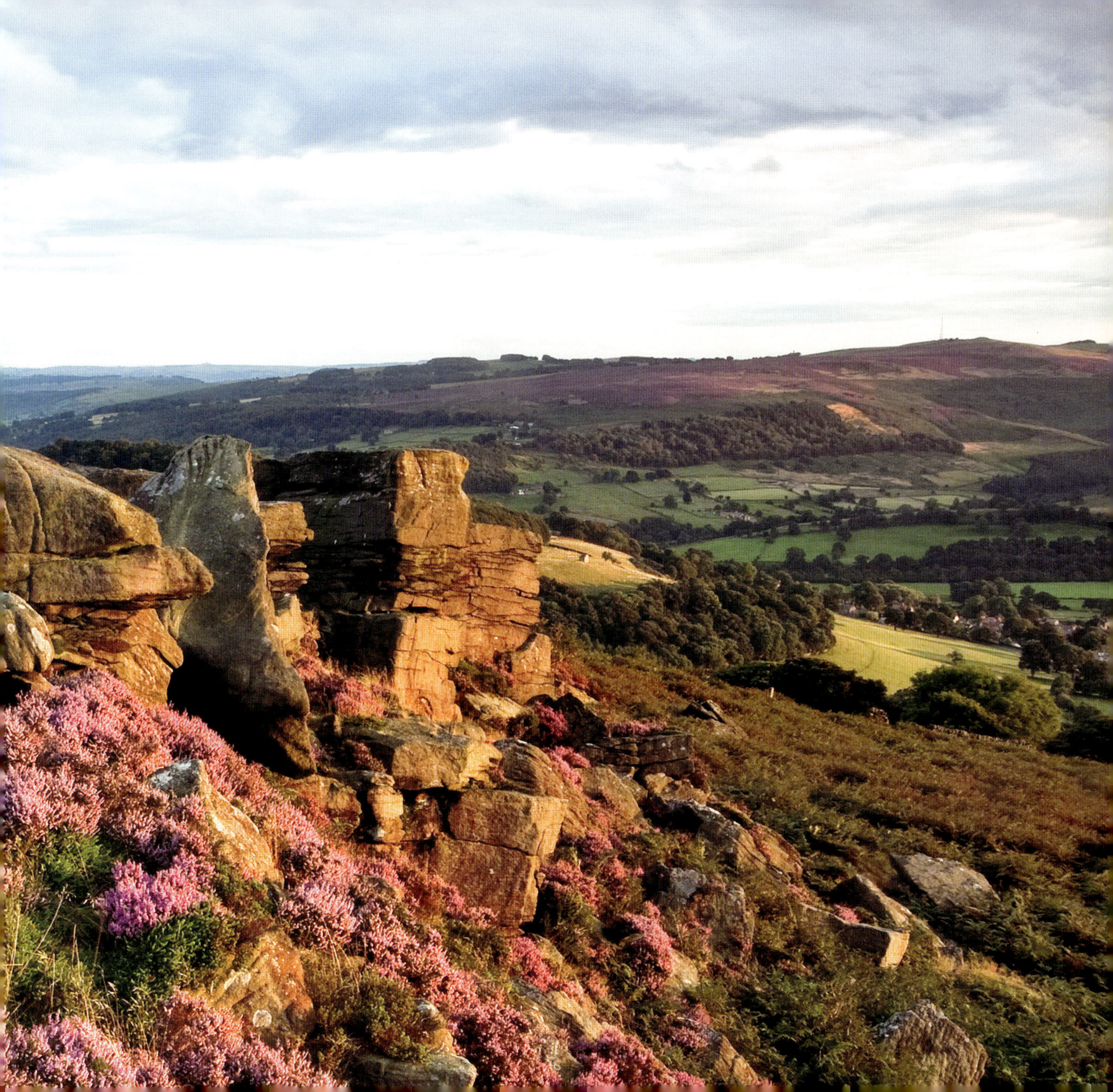

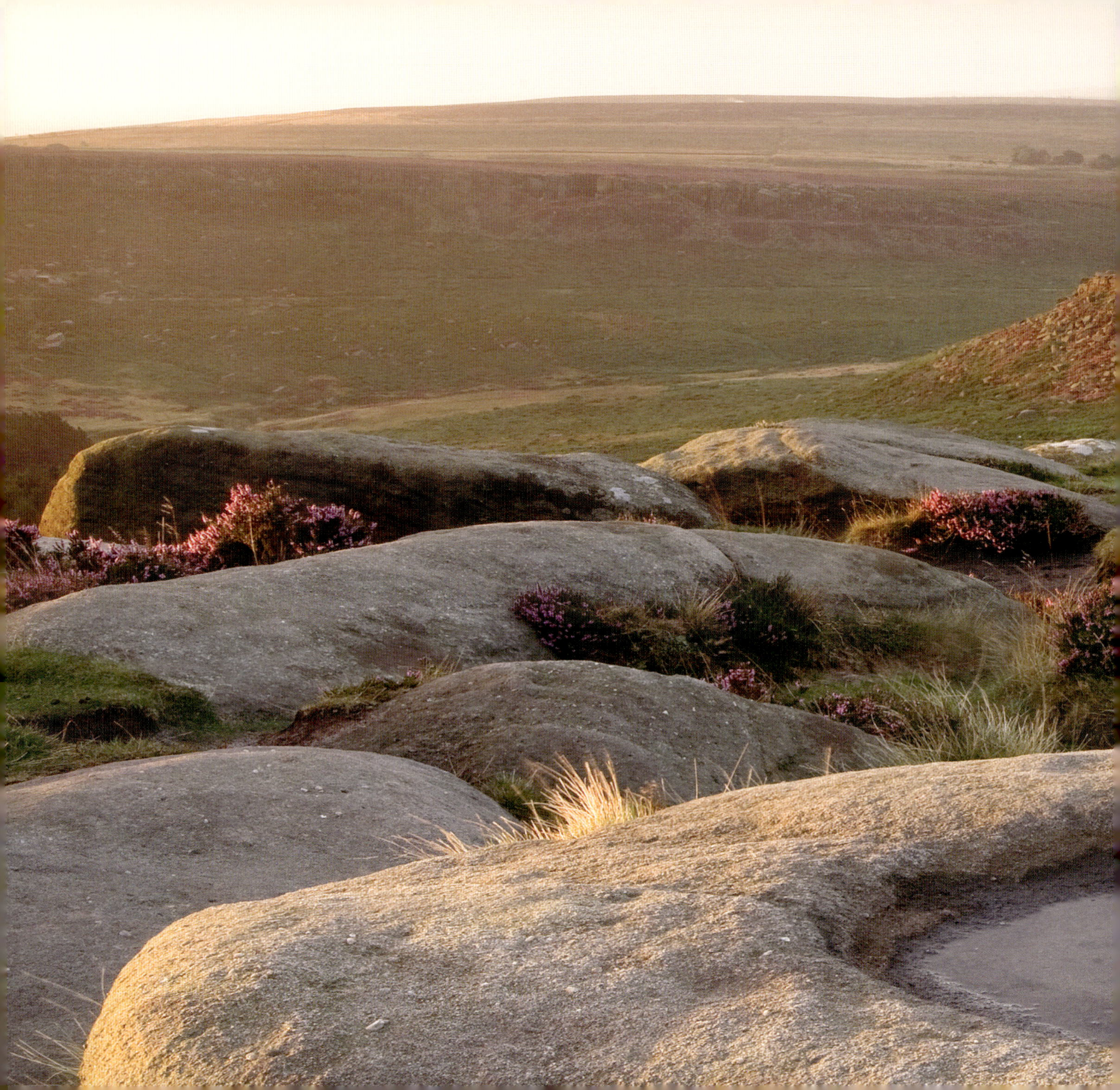

The rising sun reveals the fantastic shapes and textures in the rocks on Higger Tor.

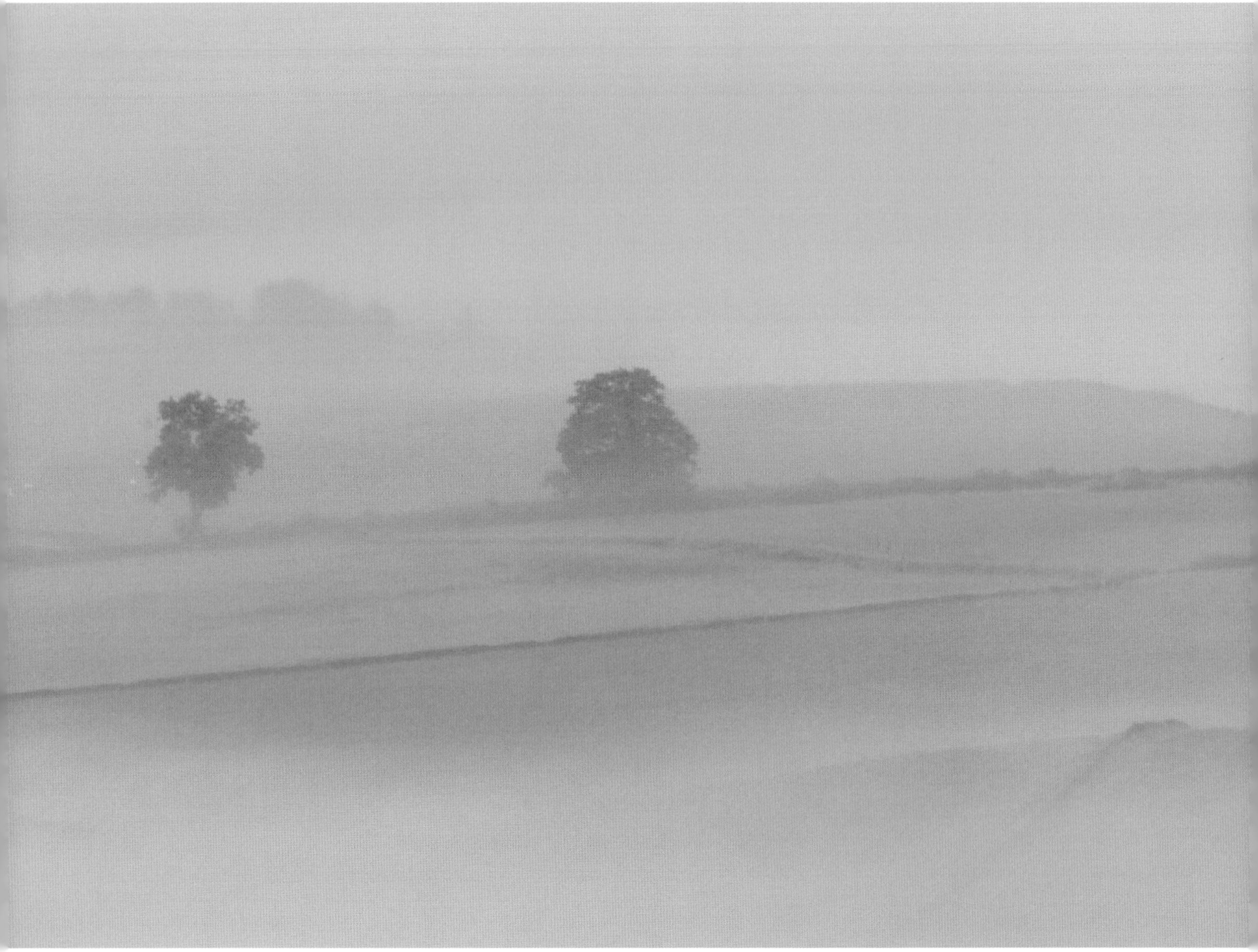

A cold summer morning is captured in this scene close to the village of Hassop. I remember this morning well as I was absolutely freezing having left my coat at home. Out of all the images I shot on this particular morning this has to be one of my favourites, it was shot about an hour before sunrise and the cold tones of the mist and pre-dawn light perfectly summed up how I was feeling at the time.

The Derwent Dams which include Howden and Derwent were constructed between 1901 and 1916 to provide water to Sheffield, Derby, Nottingham and Leicester. The project to build the dams was so large that an entire temporary village called Birchinlee was created to house the workers. This image shows the autumn colours with Howden Dam reflecting into Howden Reservoir.

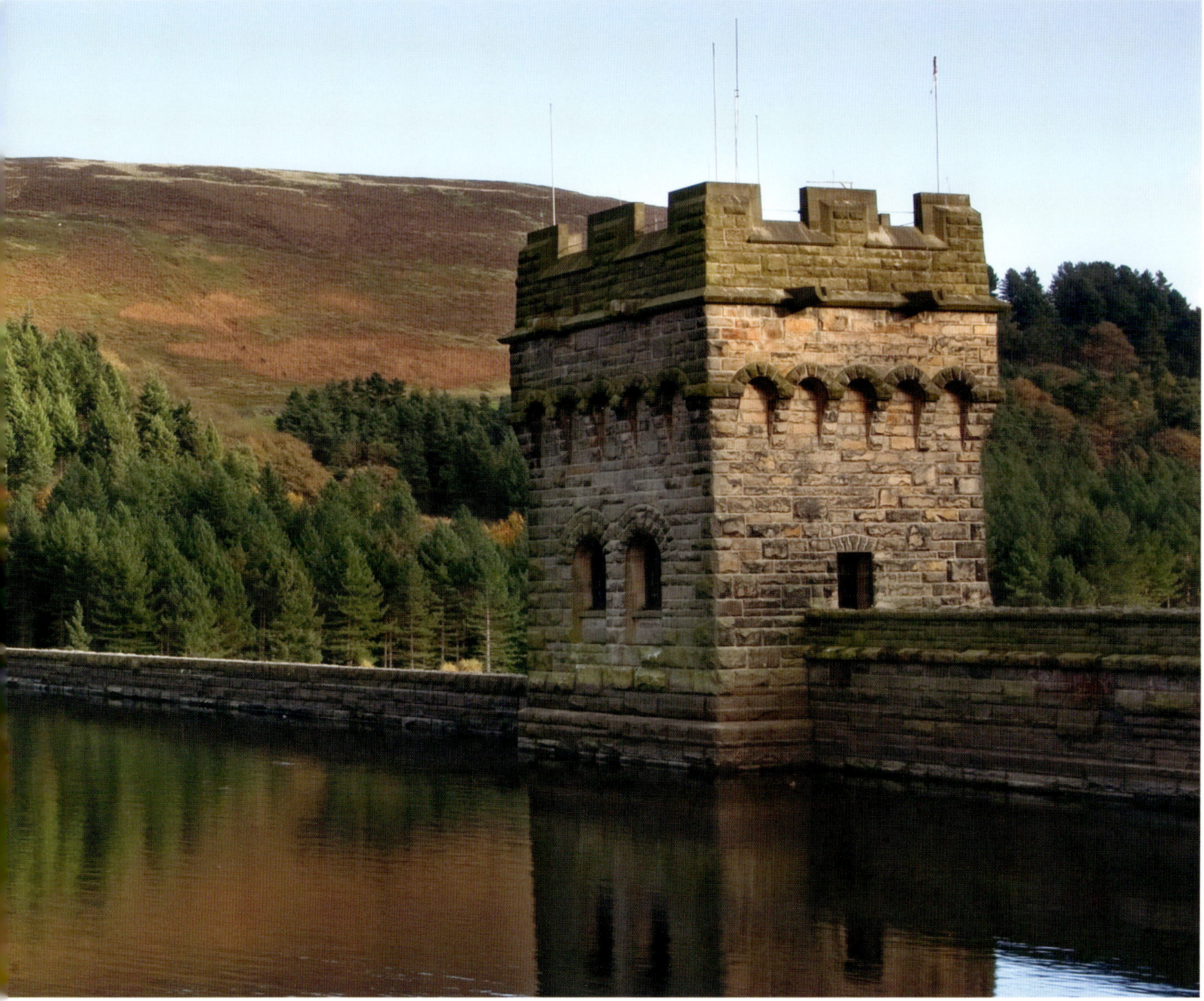

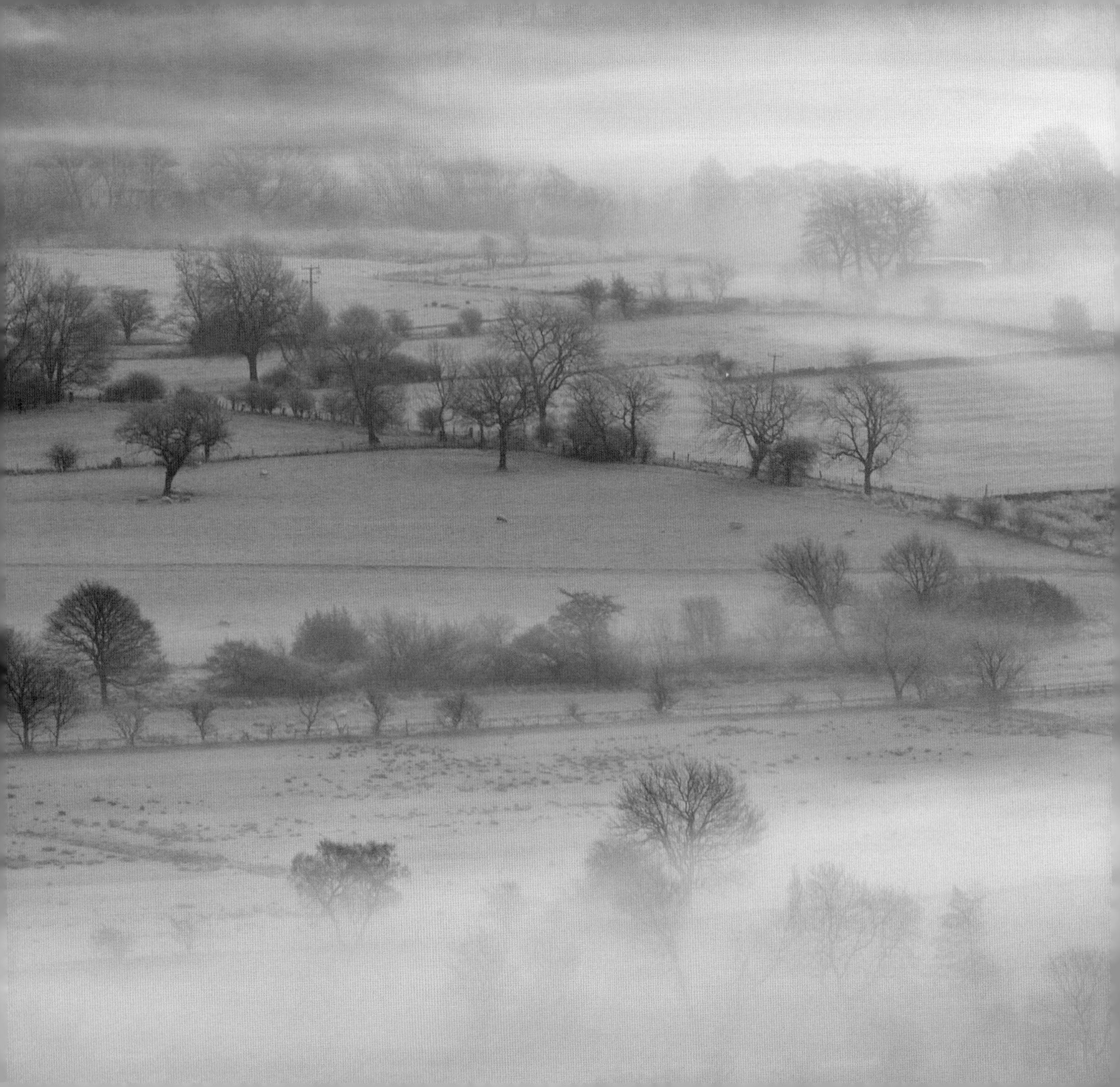

Early morning mist in the Hope Valley at dawn.

The A57 Glossop to Sheffield road is carried across Ladybower Reservoir by the Ashopton Viaduct. Built between 1935 and 1943 the building of the reservoir resulted in the flooding of the villages of Derwent and Ashopton. During extra dry spells it's still possible to see the remains of the flooded Derwent village.

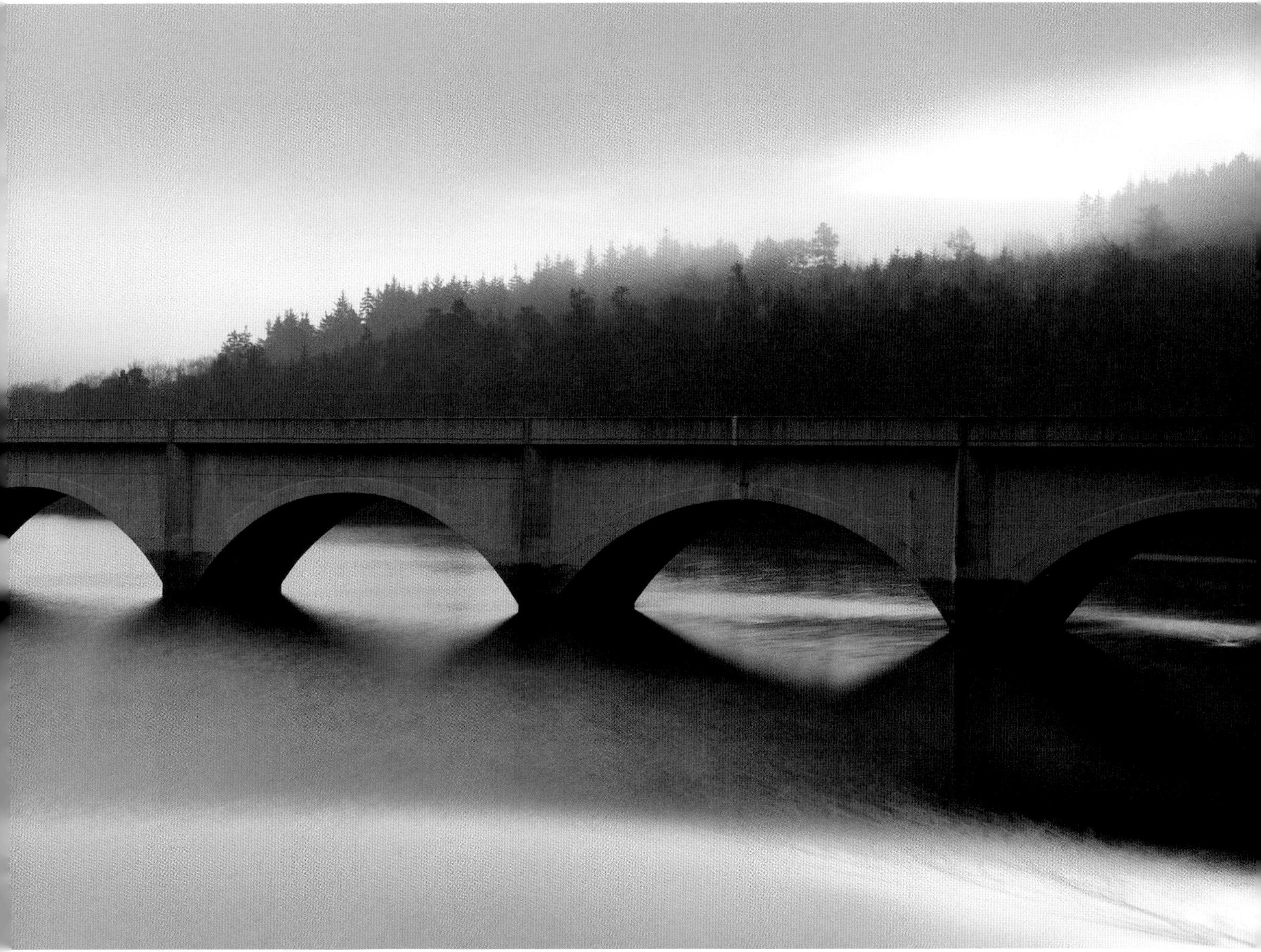

Whilst driving around chasing the disappearing mist at sunrise I stumbled across this wonderful autumn picture close to the village of Bamford. I was not only drawn to this scene by the autumn colours I also loved the way the road snaked its way through the landscape.

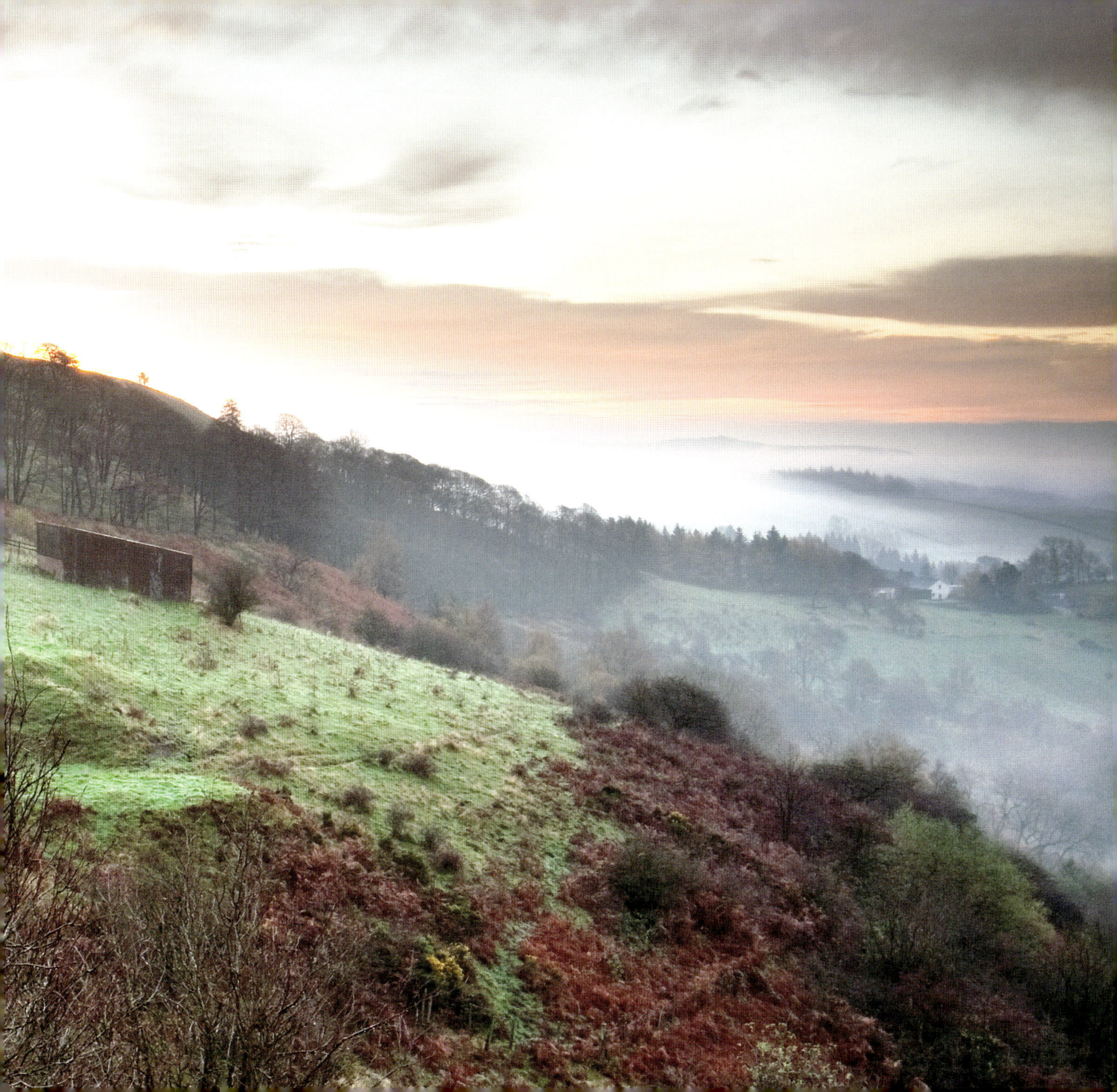

The vibrant autumn colours of Padley Gorge seen here on a foggy October morning.

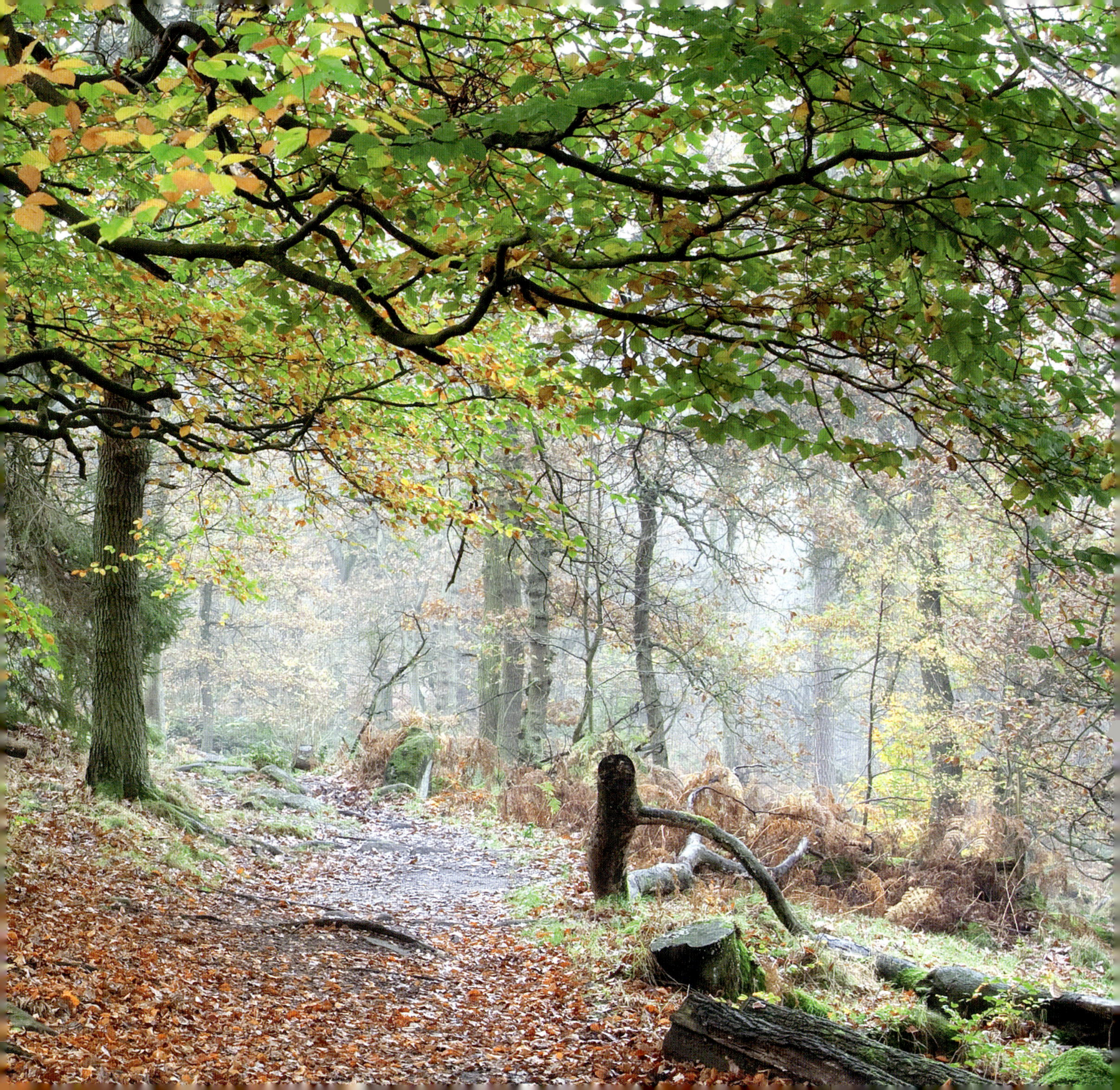

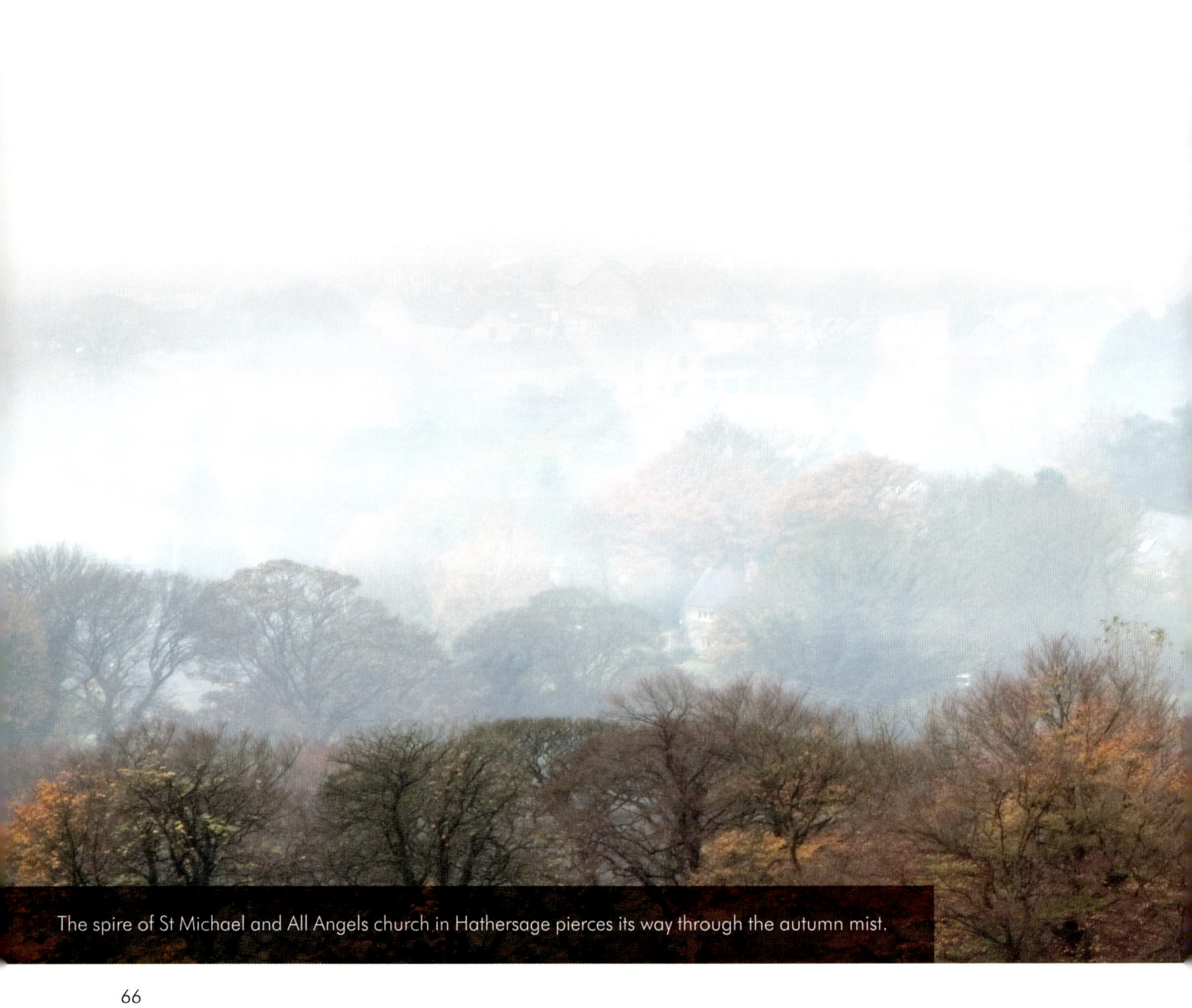

The spire of St Michael and All Angels church in Hathersage pierces its way through the autumn mist.

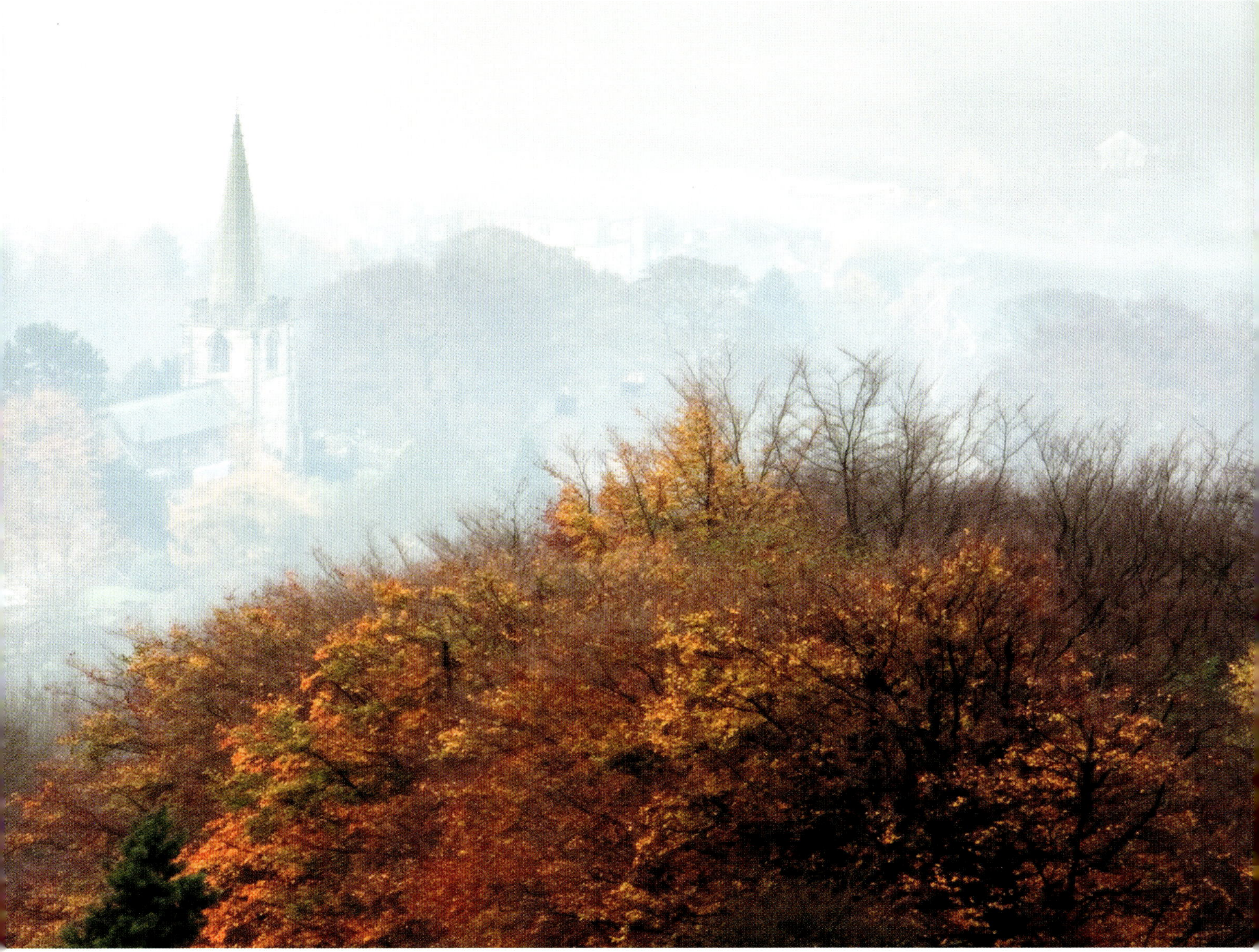

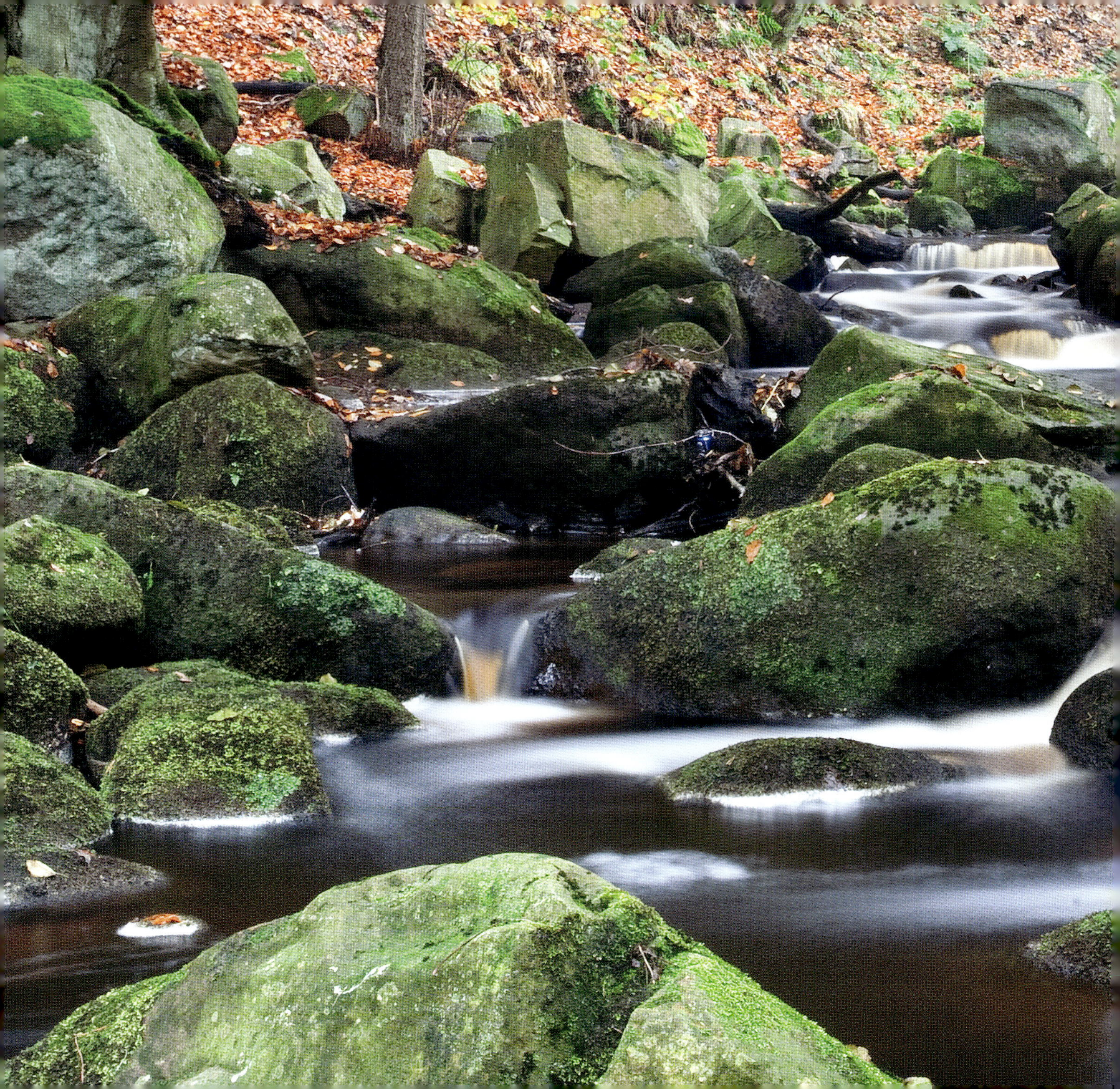

Every year the autumn colours of Padley Gorge attract visitors from all over the country. What I personally love most about this place is the fantastic brown stained colour of the water caused by the peat through which it is filtered.

This fallow deer was captured during the autumn rut. The backlighting from the rising sun really helps to show off the body heat of this impressive buck.

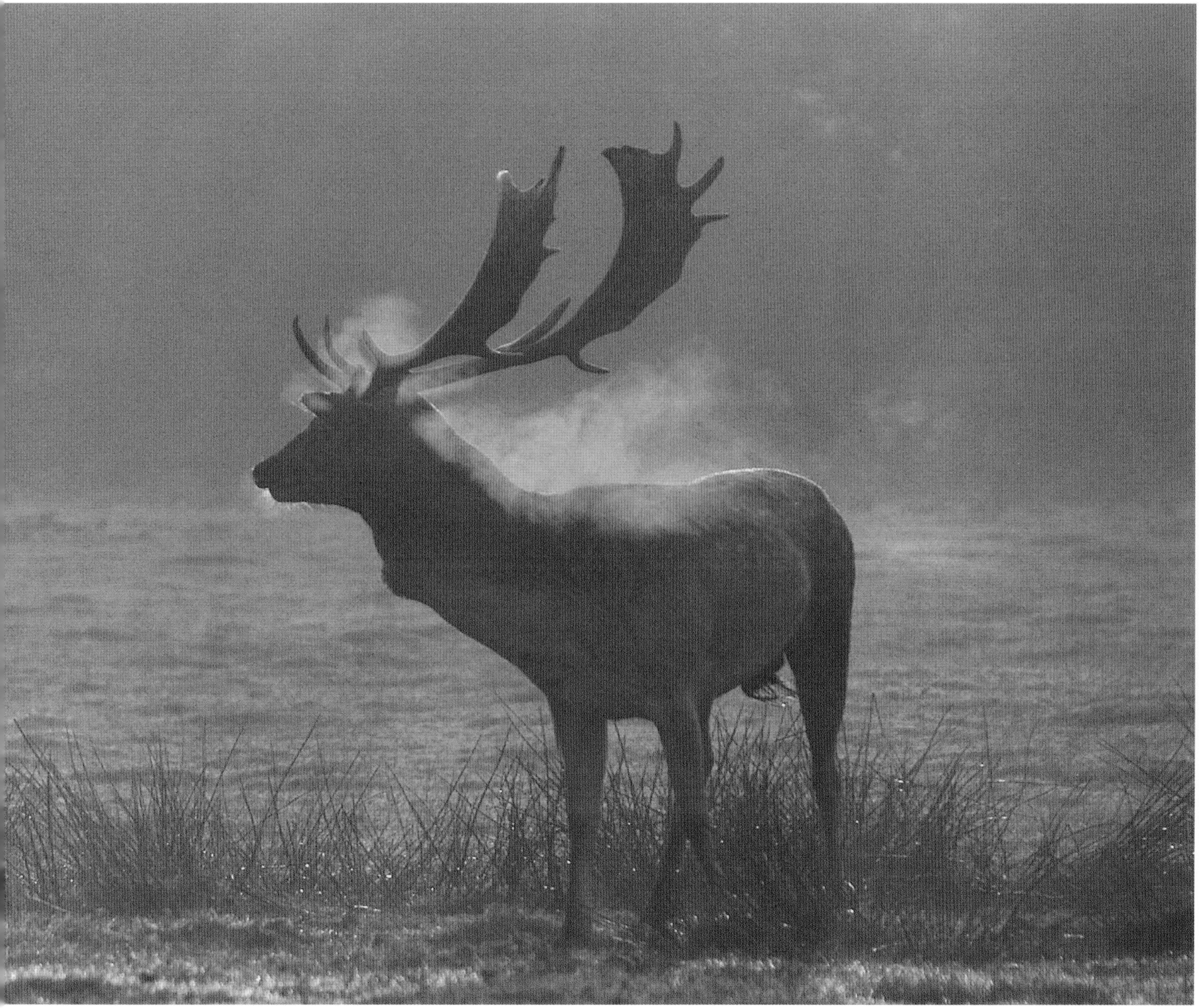

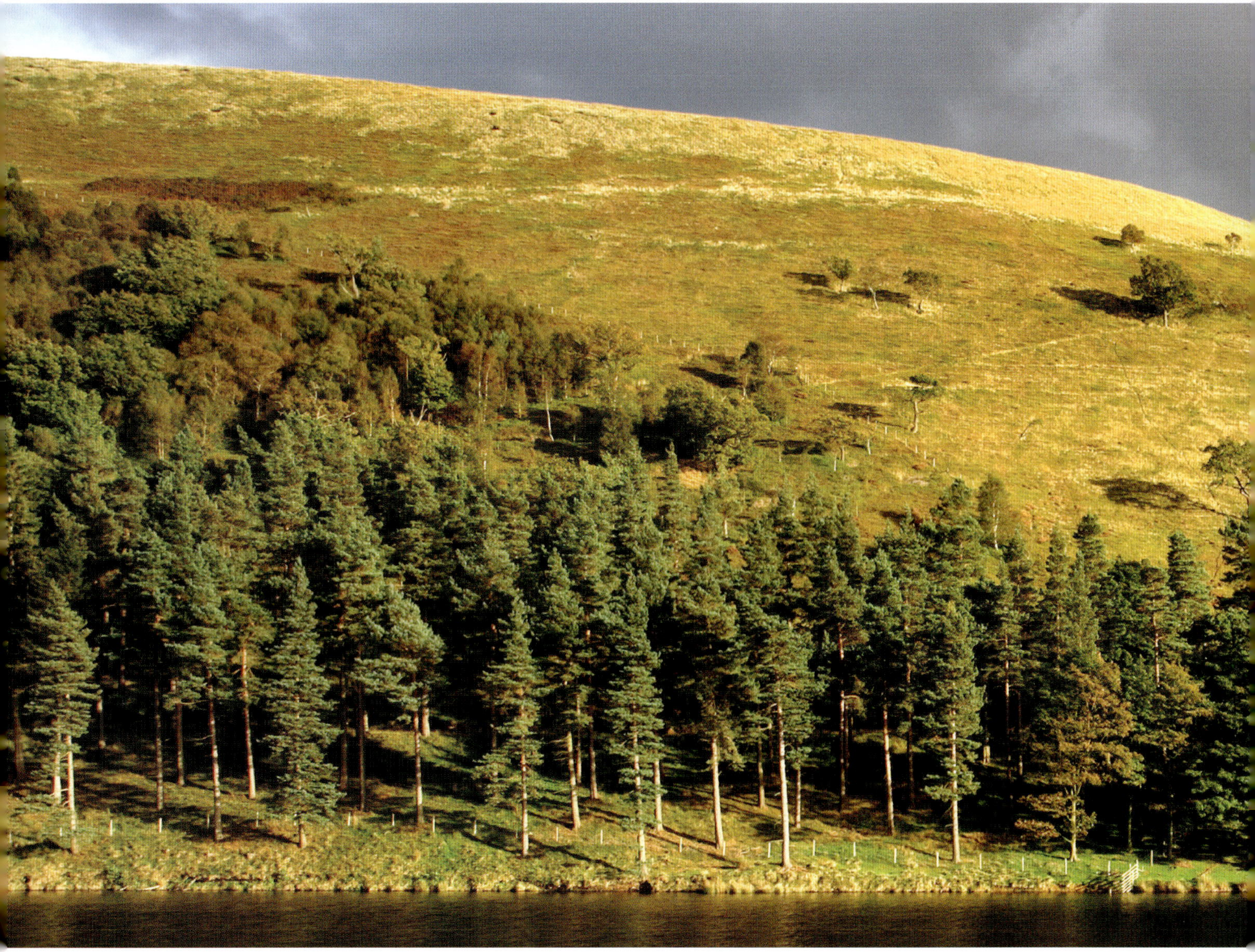

Pine trees reflecting in Derwent Reservoir during a passing storm in the Upper Derwent Valley.

An abandoned millstone adds some extra interest to this scene in Padley Gorge.

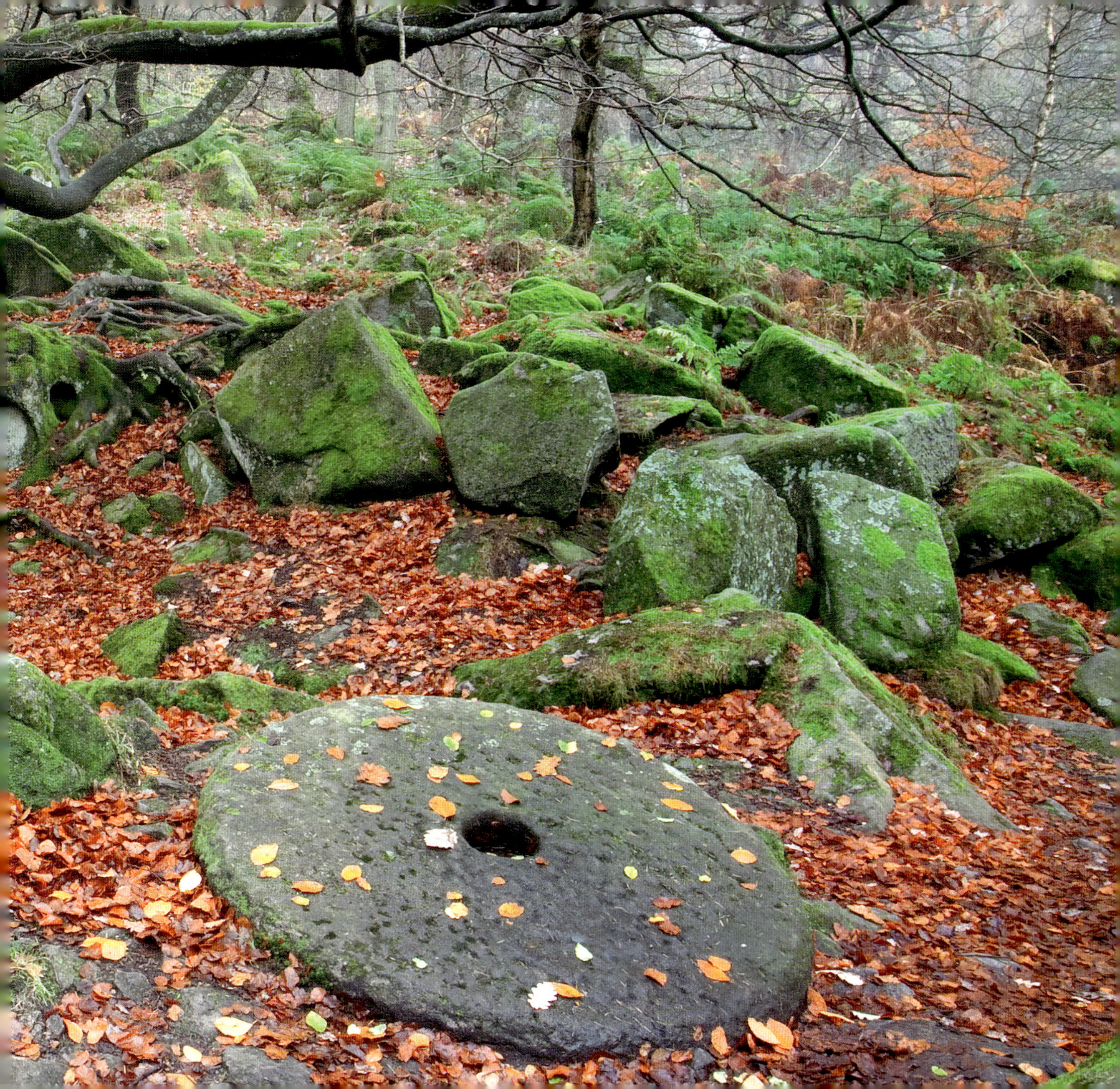

The Hope Valley Cement Works shrouded in dawn mist.

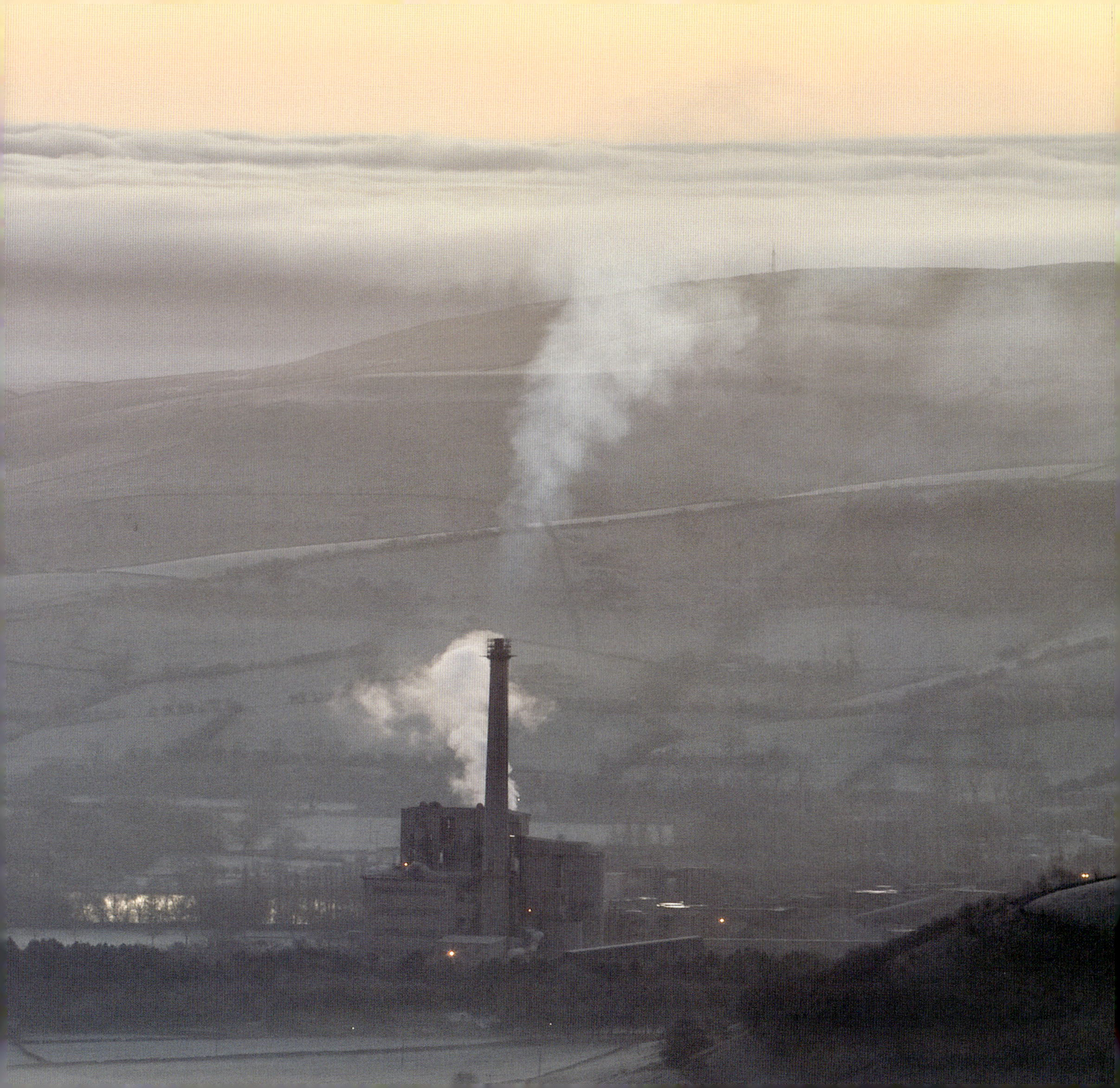

Abandoned millstones such as these located beneath the southern edge of Stanage Edge can be found all over this area of the Peak District. Millstone production was once one of the major industries in the Peak District until cheaper imports from the continent meant the industry collapsed in the nineteenth century.

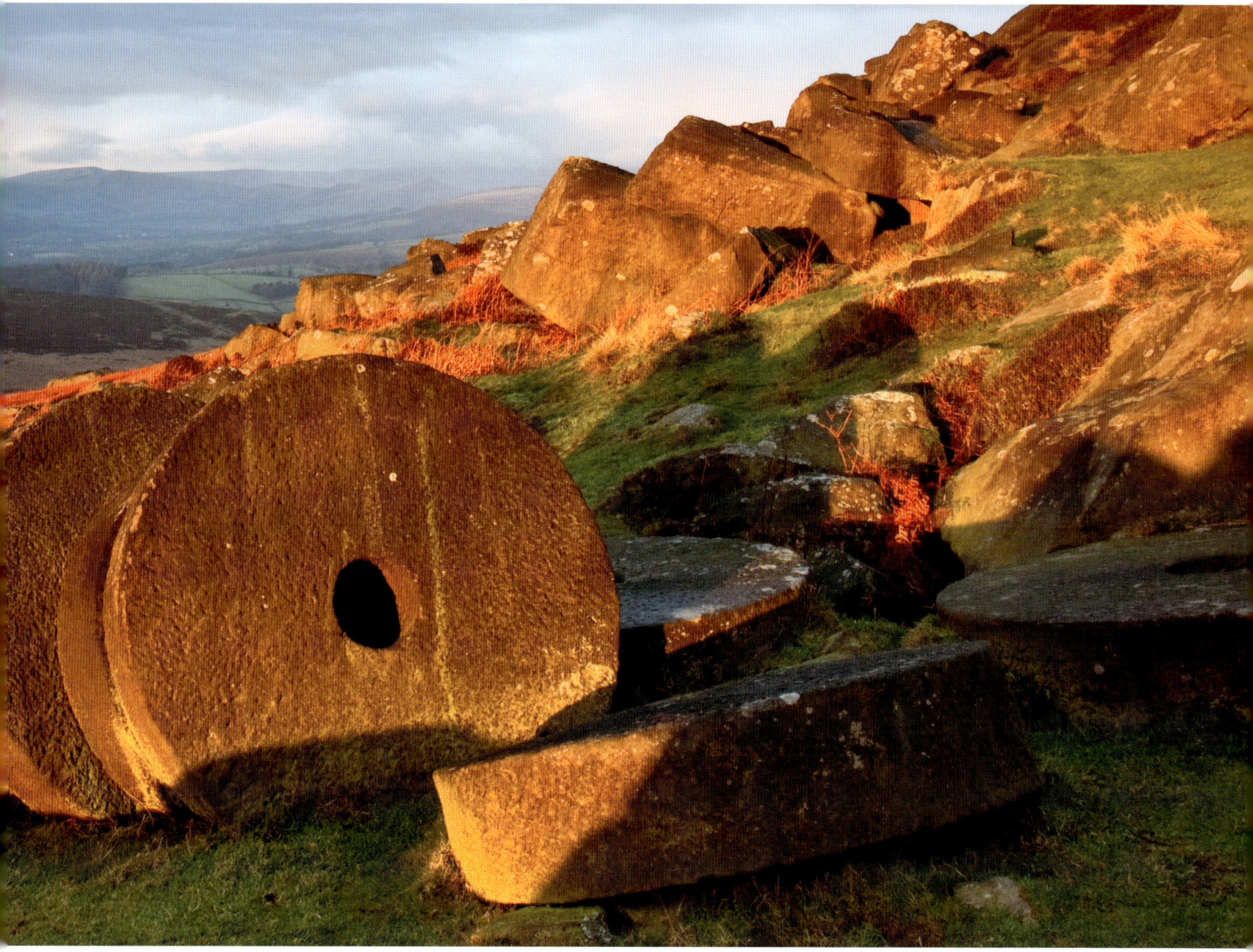

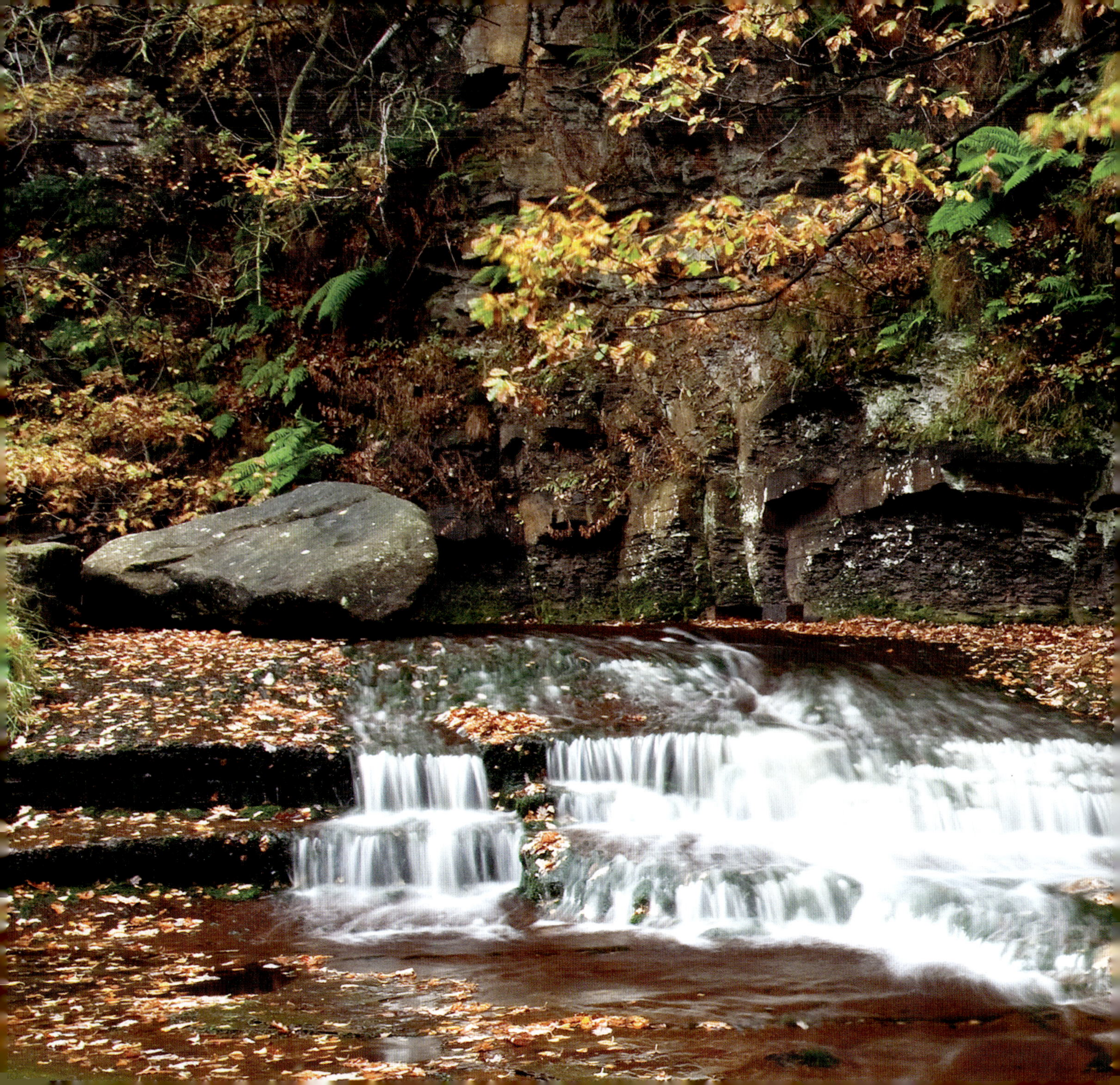

The little known Black Clough that runs off of Bleaklow has some of the finest waterfalls in the Peak District. When the colourful autumn leaves start to fall this becomes one of the most beautiful spots in the whole of the Peak District.

Mam Tor dominates the head of the Hope Valley. The name Mam Tor literally translates as heights of the mother. Due to the crumbling nature of its east face it is also known locally as 'The Shivering Mountain'.

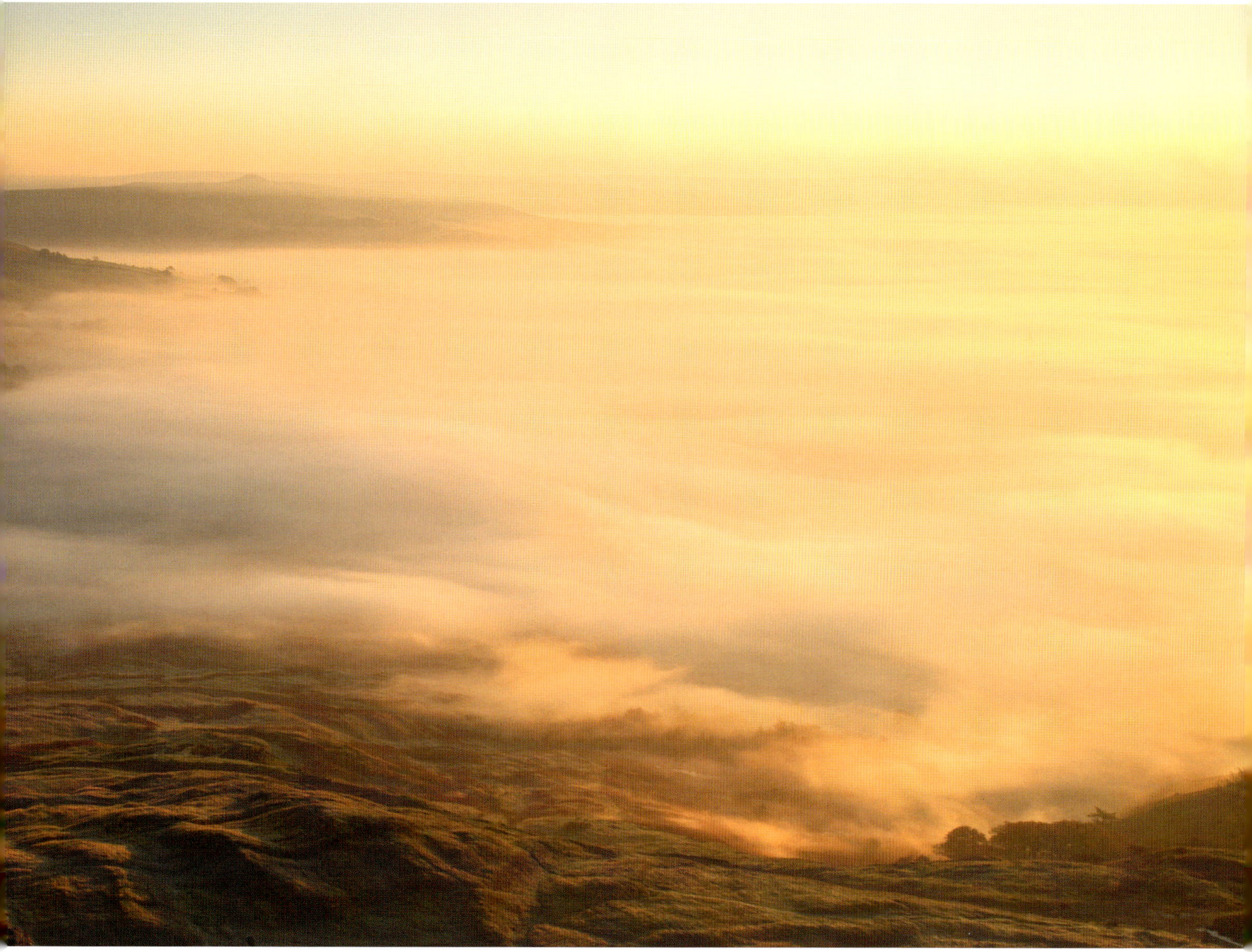

A cloud invasion rolls over the hills of Lose Hill and Back Tor on a frosty winter's morning.

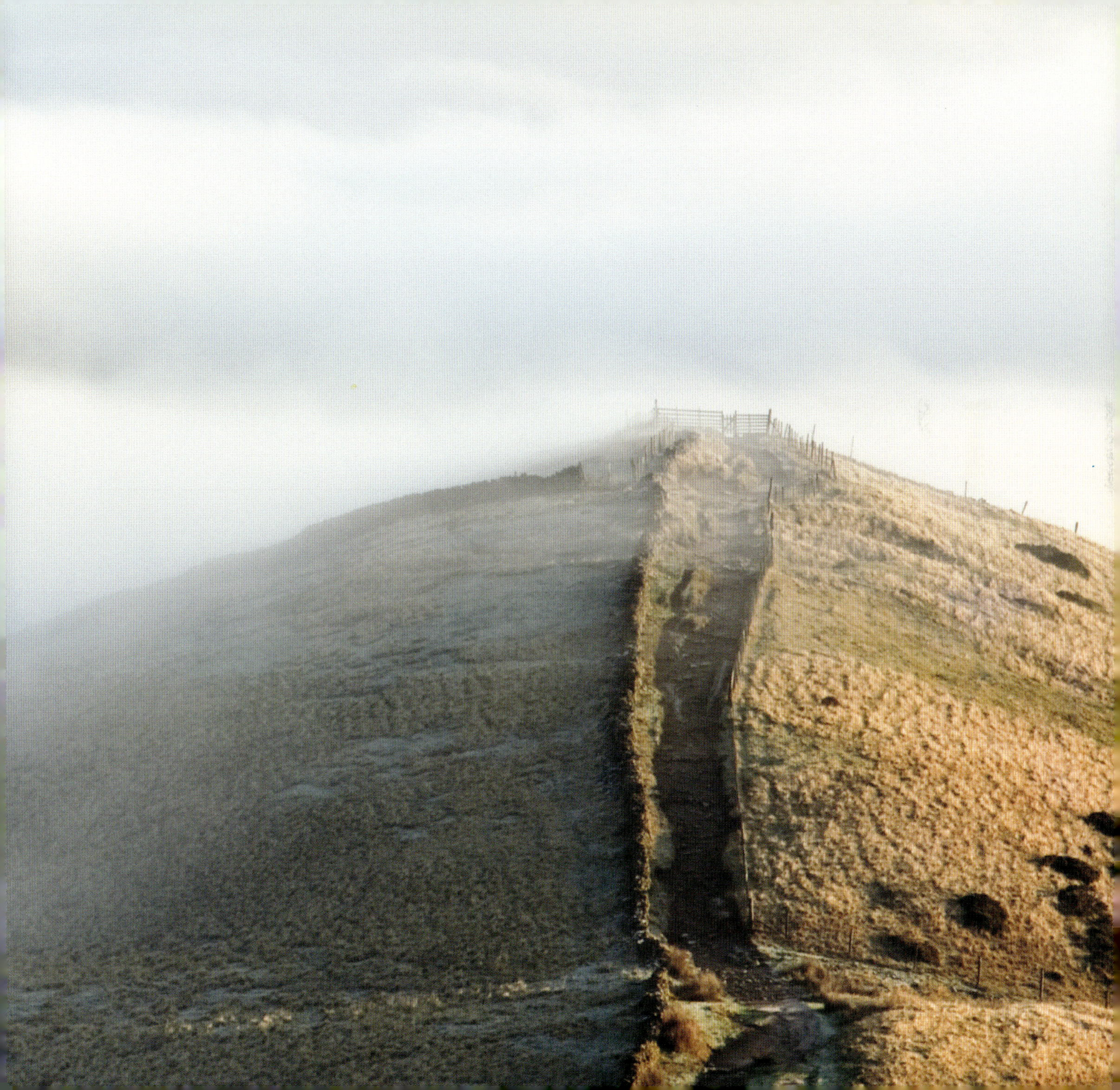

A flat calm afternoon on Ladybower Reservoir following light winter snowfall.

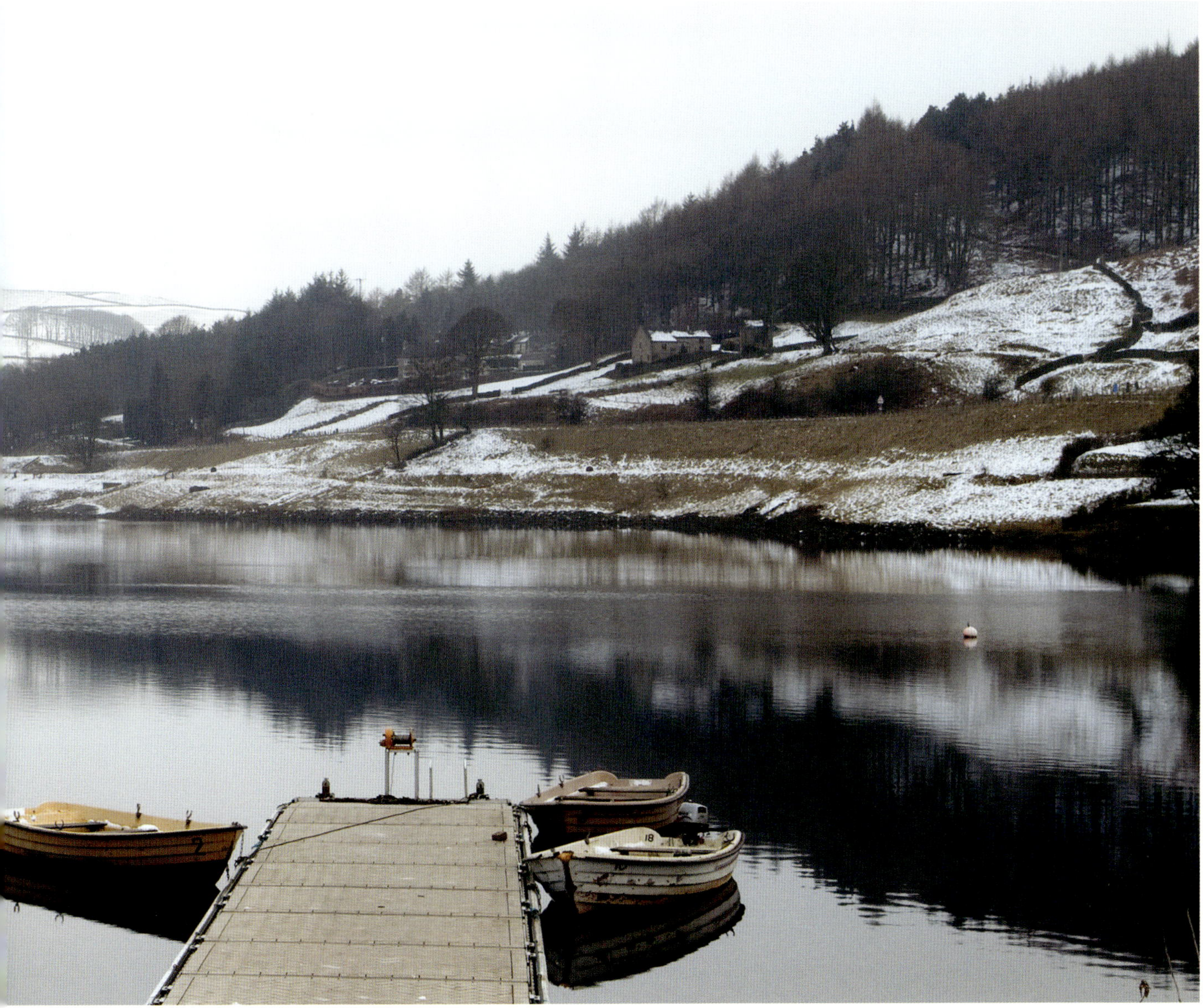

& Bar
Ensuite
Olde Nag's Head
Hotel
Tel: 01433 620 248
Ye Olde Nag's Head
Hot and Cold Food
Served All Day Everyday
CROSS ST
TO LET

At Christmas the popular village of Castleton takes on a magical feel once dusk arrives and the beautiful Christmas lights decorate the High Street.

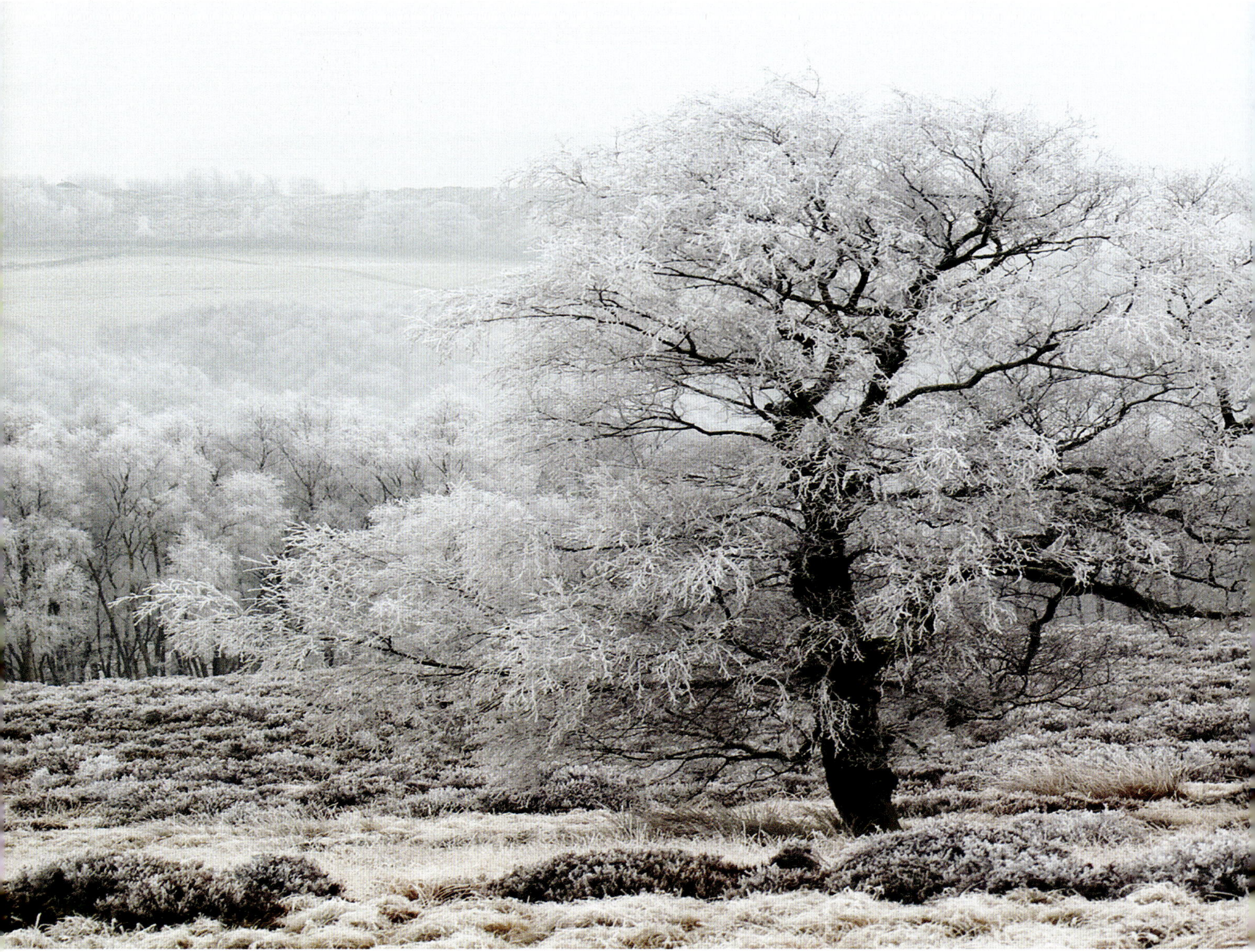

A spectacular overnight hoar frost as a result of freezing fog left tiny delicate ice crystals all over this landscape on Lawrence Field looking towards Padley Gorge.

Late afternoon light adds a warm glow to the rocks and snow on Curbar Edge as a family gathers in the distance to watch the setting sun.

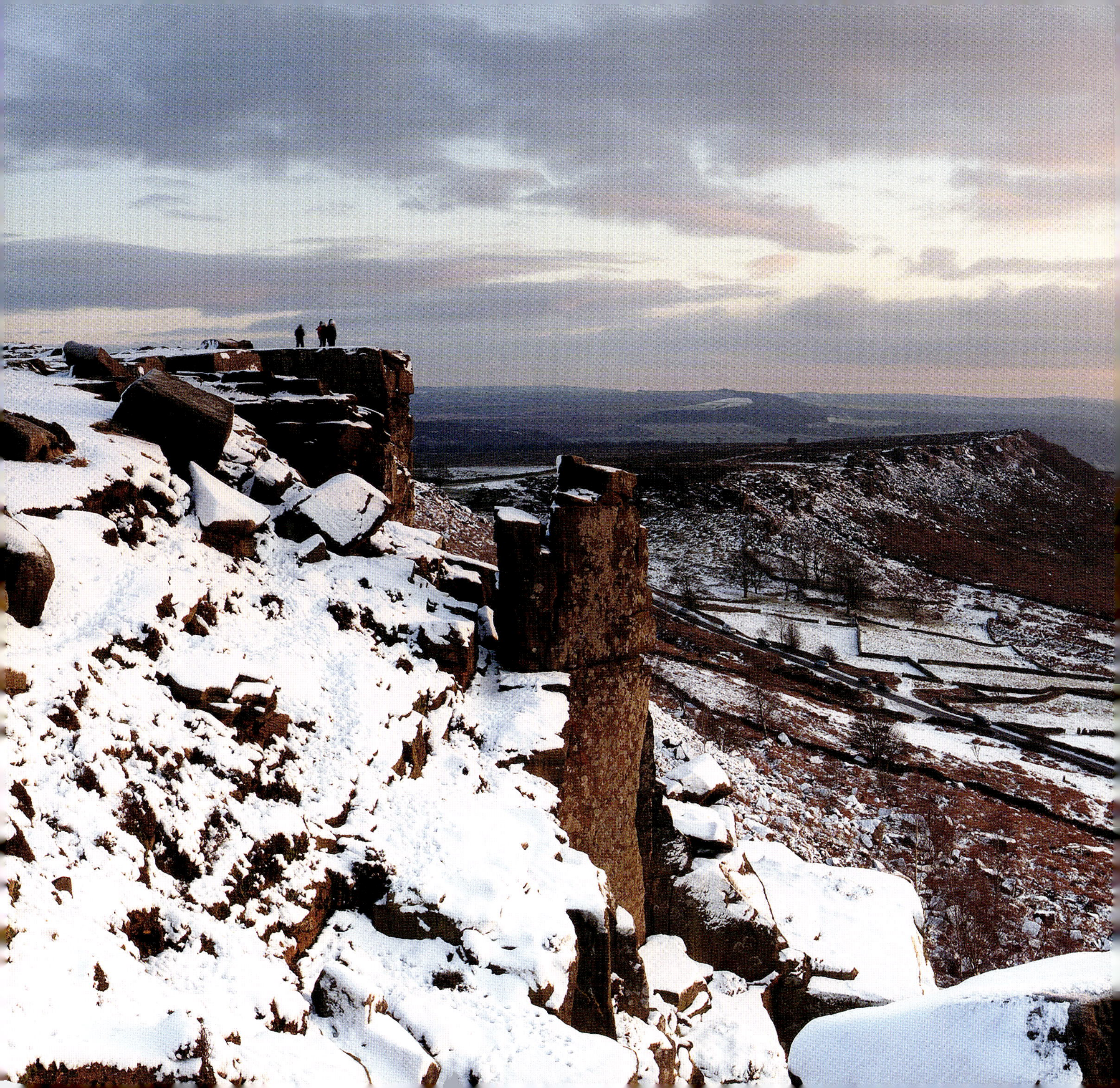

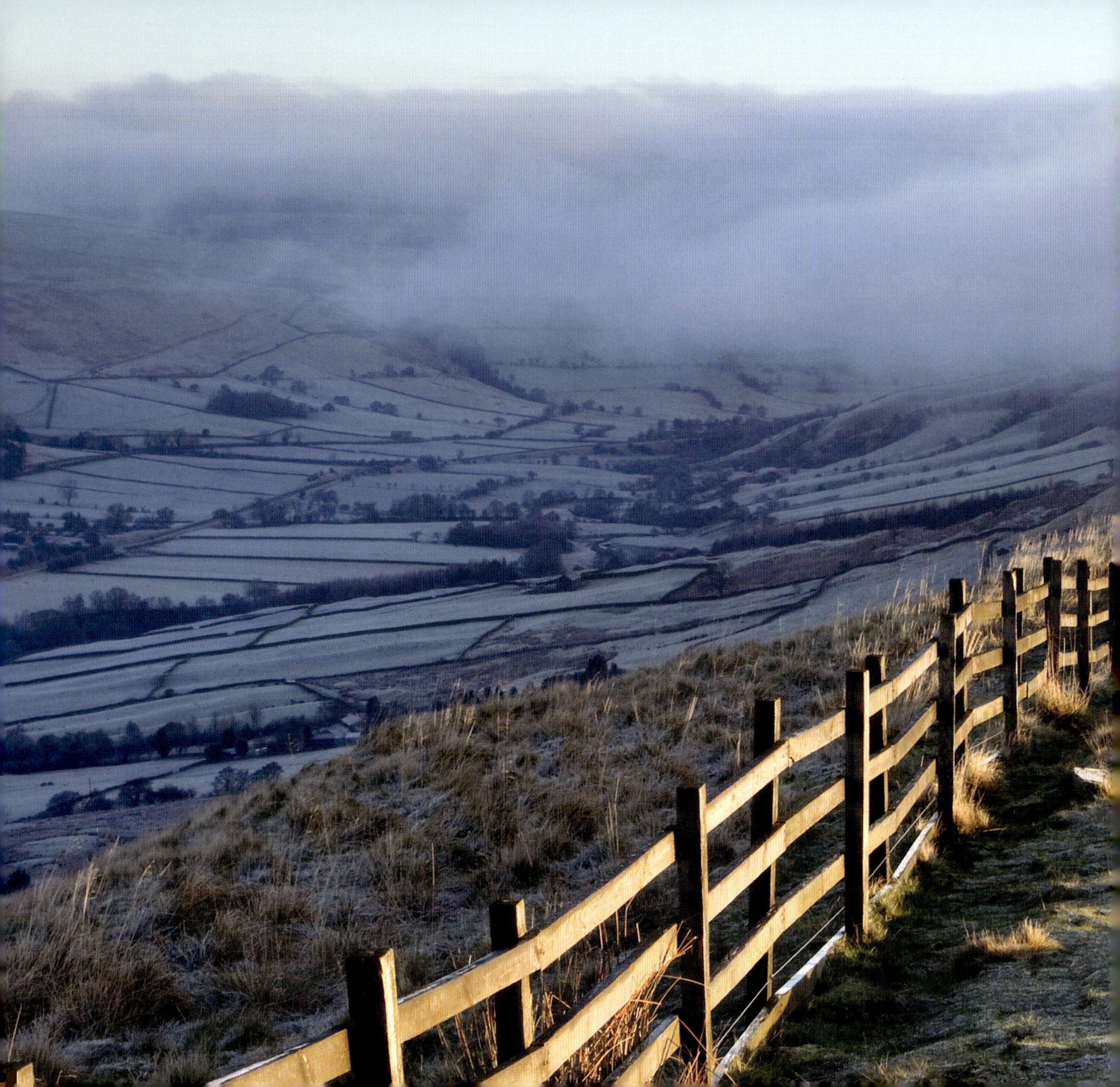

The great ridge on a cold and frosty morning with the Edale Valley to the left.

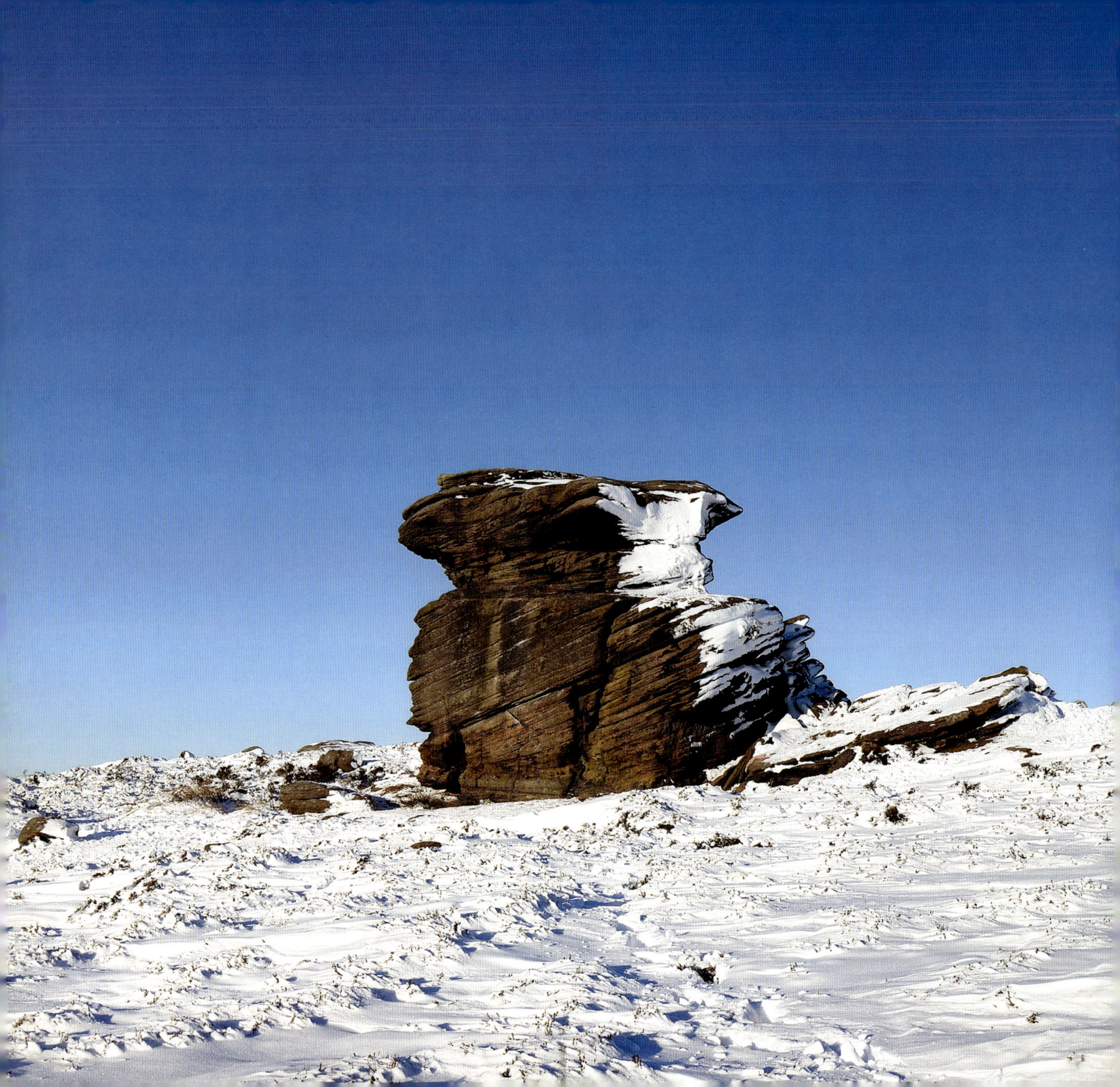

Mother Cap on Owler Moor captured following days of heavy winter snowfall in the winter of 2010.

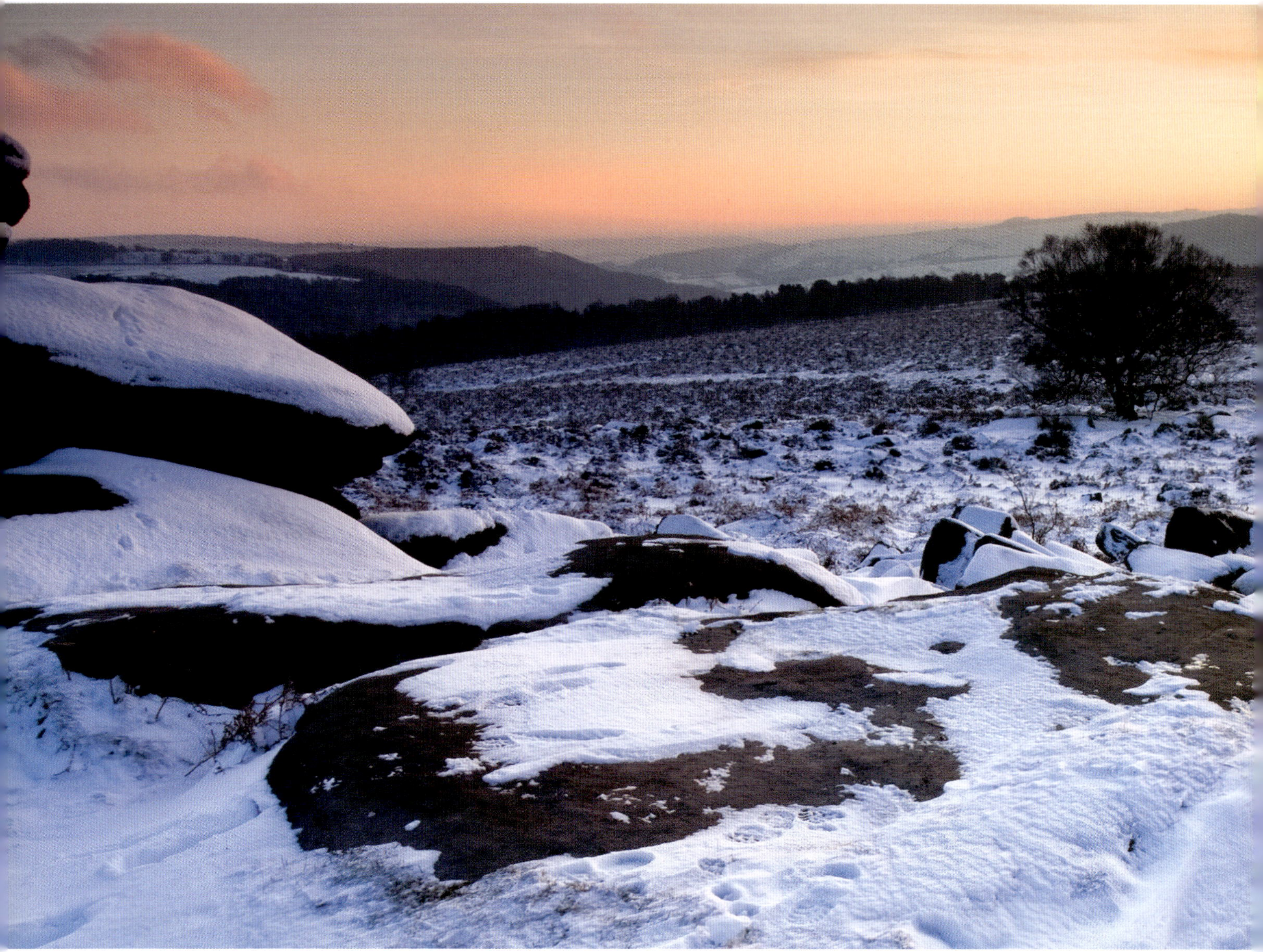

A colourful winter sunset is captured here from the rocks on Over Owler Tor.

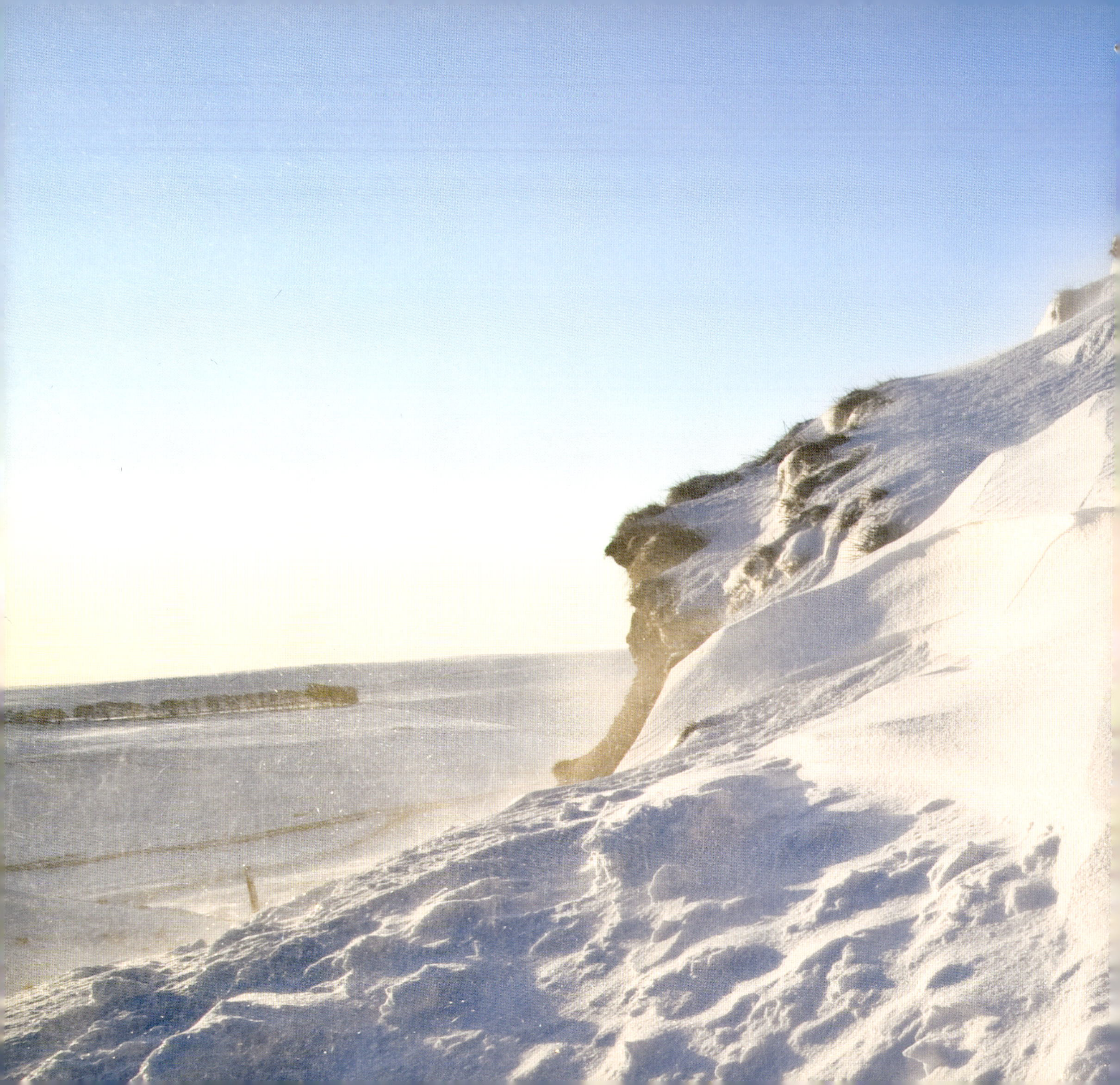

Fascinating snow patterns caused by the strong winds are illuminated by the morning sun on Rushup Edge.

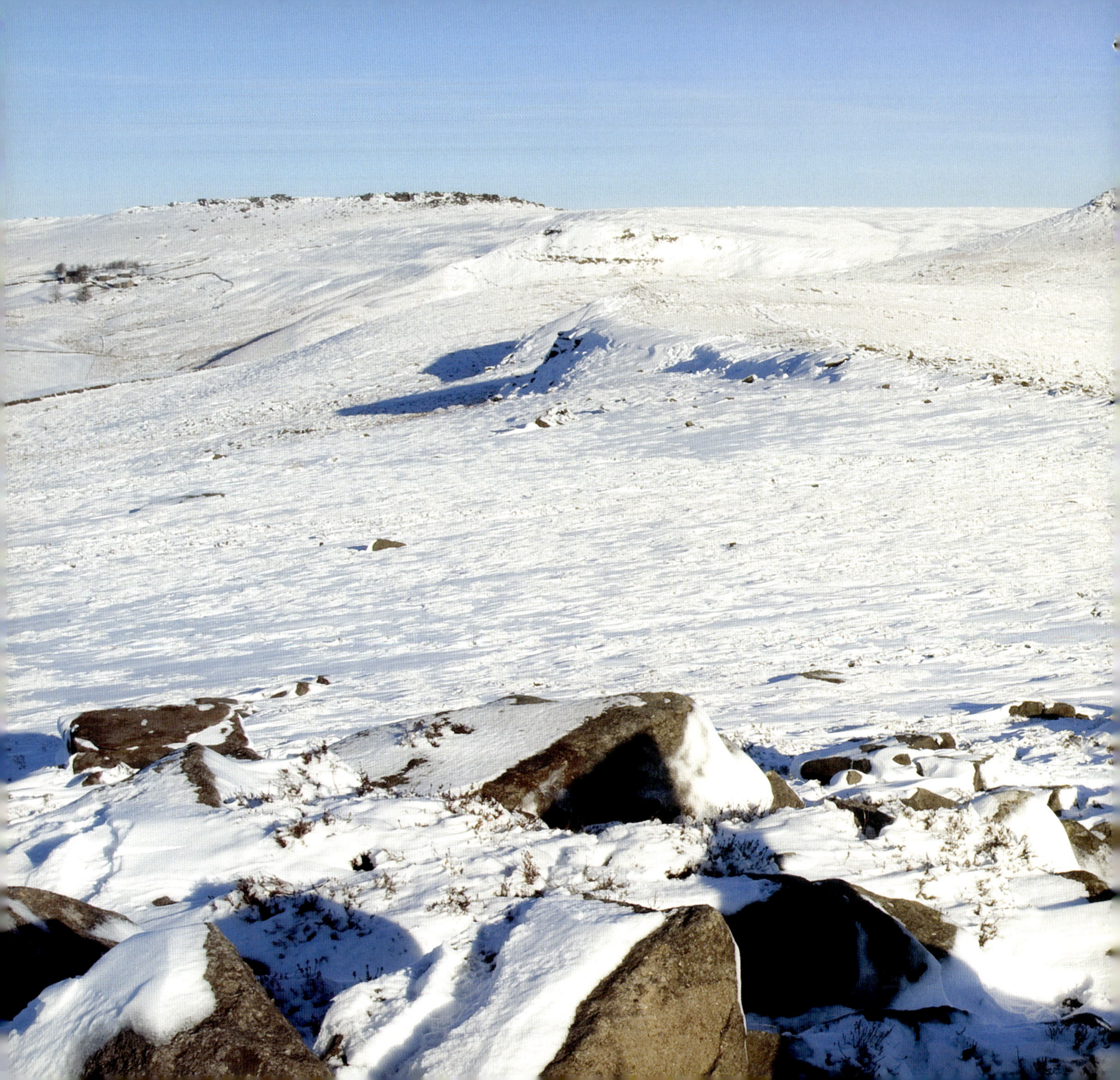

Over Owler Tor looking towards Higger Tor on a glorious winter's morning.

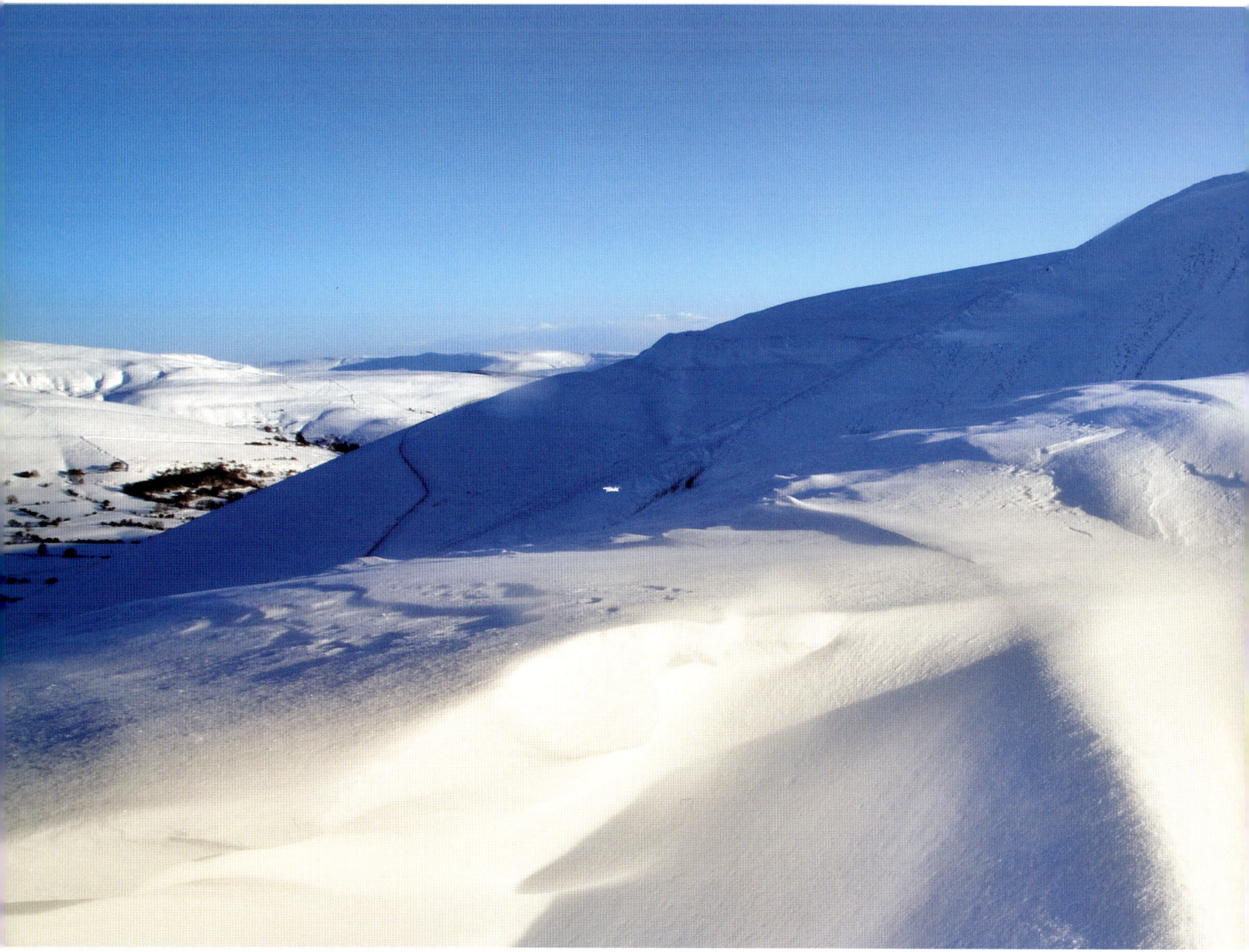

Days of heavy snow and strong winds left knee-deep snow deposits on top of Rushup Edge on a bright but extremely cold winter morning. In the background the high point of Mam Tor can be seen.

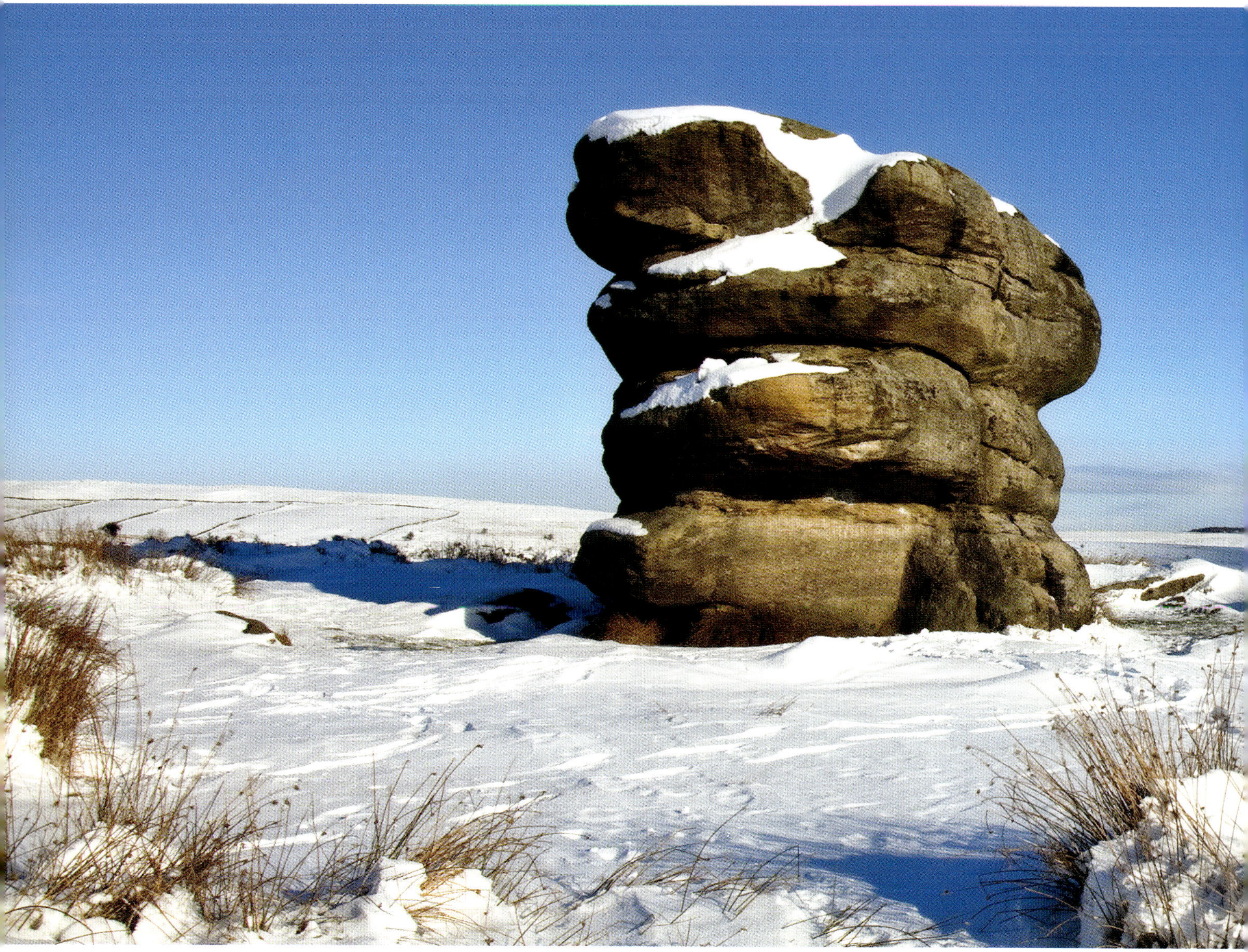

The Eagle Stone is a large weathered rock close to the eastern end of Baslow Edge. Local folklore states that the men of Baslow once had to climb the stone before they were eligible to marry.

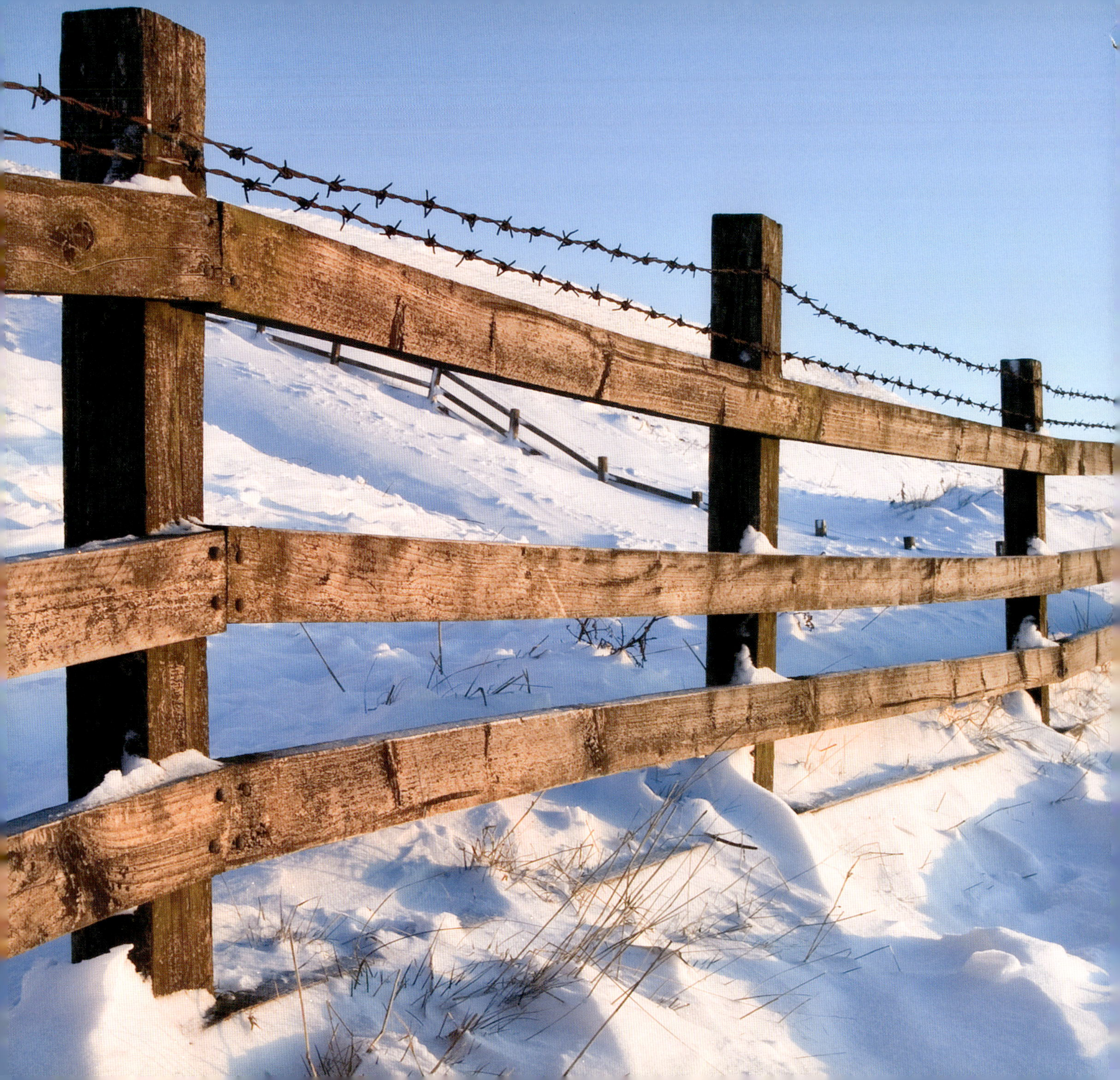

This rising sun deceptively adds some warm light to this scene on the lower slopes of Mam Tor. Whilst the colour of the light may have been warm the temperature at -12 certainly was not.

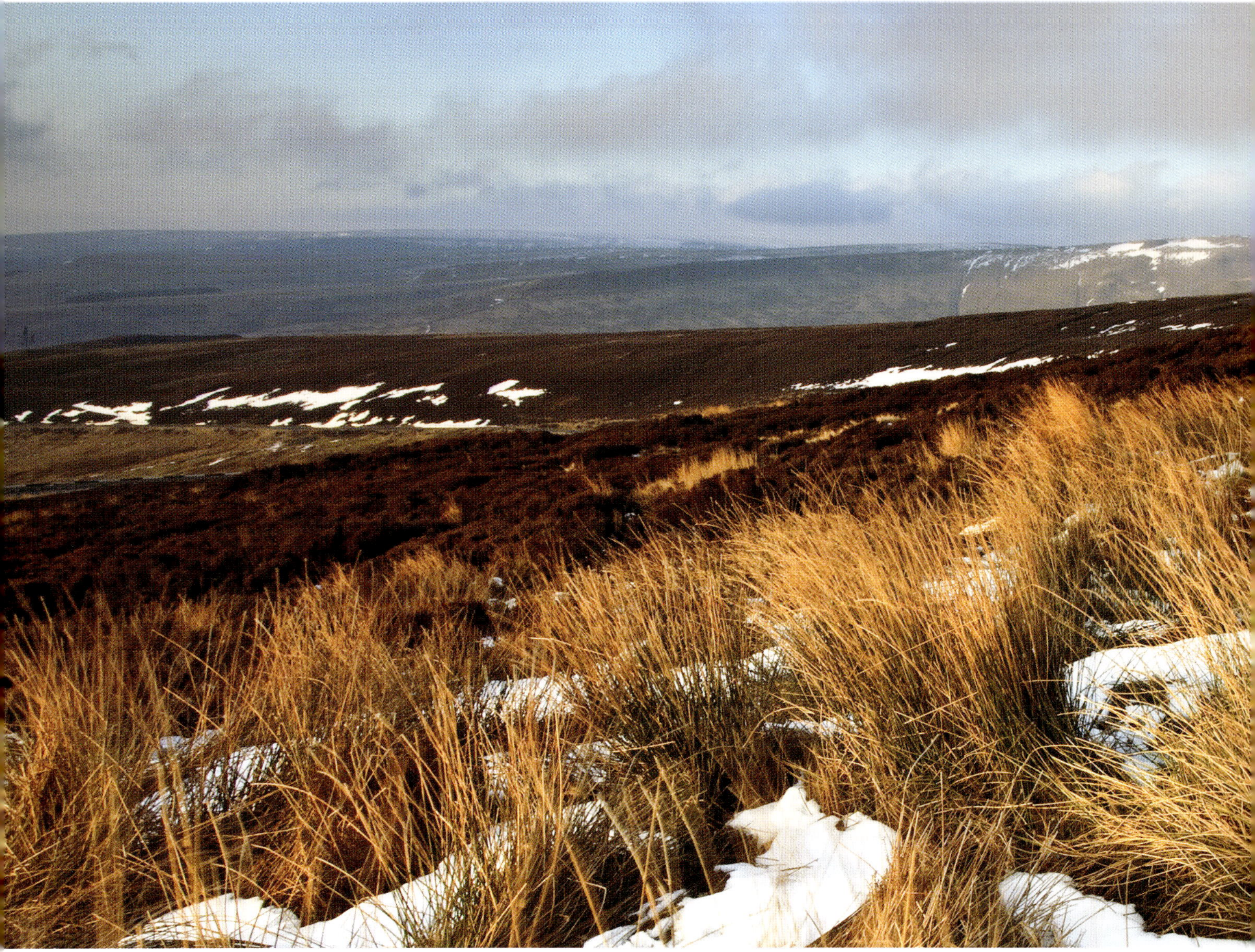

Patches of winter snow hang on to the slopes of Bleaklow. Bleaklow is the northern sister of nearby Kinder made up of large areas of deep peat.

The unusual position that this exposed tree grows in shows you what the weather can be like on Rushup Edge at times. The tree has had to adapt to its surroundings and has grown into a position where it is almost trying to use the slope of Rushup Edge to help protect it from the strong winds. At most times of the year you would still be able to see plenty of clearance between the trunk and the slope itself however on this occasion the snow was so deep the majority of the trunk has disappeared under the snow.